ACTION FIGURES & TOY

ACTION JOE
THE STORY OF THE FRENCH GI JOE

Erwan LE VEXIER

Translated from the French by Hazel GAVIGNIAUX

All the original photos, which illustrate this book, have been produced by Erwan Le Vexier at La Reverse (for the outdoors) and in the studio of grenierajouets.com (for the indoors) between May 2001 and June 2004 (all rights reserved).
Erwan Le Vexier has produced some supplementary photos in the Editor's studio of Dixième Planète.
The images of the epoch from the catalogues and publicity (all rights reserved) come from Author's personal archives.
Extracts from Philippe L'Helgoualc'h's conversation with Erwan Le Vexier in July 2004.
All the toys seen in this book come from Erwan Le Vexier's personal collection, except for the James Bond *Action Man*, which was lent by *Hasbro France*, two 1976 advertisements on page 65, which come from Jean-Marc Deschamps' collection and the 1965 advertisement of *GI Joe*, which comes from Jean-Claude Piffret's archives.

Action Joe, Group Action Joe, GI Joe, Action Man are trademarks of Hasbro International Inc.

HISTOIRE & COLLECTIONS

Forty years ago, in 1964, Hasbro created GI Joe, the first 'doll for boys'. His size of 12-inches, his numerous articulations and realistic accessories rapidly made him the modern reference in the toy world.

Best known in Europe under the name *Action Man*, this articulated adventurer was exploited under various names throughout the world. In France, it was *Action Joe* from 1976 to 1981.

BEFORE ACTION JOE (1964-75) 8

ACTION JOE (1976-81)
    The six glorious years 10
    Comrades in adventure 16

    A whole world of adventures 26
        Military 28
        Adventure 38
        Wild West 46
        Outer Space 52

    Technical analysis 58

    The communication
        Stars & Competitions 62
        Advertising 64

AFTER ACTION JOE (1982-2004) 70

THE OTHER COUNTRIES AND INSPIRATIONS 76

INDEX 80

5

GROUP ACTION JOE
ceji arbois
MUSTANG
7960
HEVAL ARTICULÉ
RNACHEMENT COMPLET
SONNAGE NON INCLUS
GARÇON
ACCESSOIRES
UTHENTIQUES
POUR GRAND
CHEF INDIEN
7926
TOM
7566
ANOË
3725
VRAI CANOË DU GROUP ACTION JOE
ECORER EN VERSION INDIEN
AGE 6-13 ANS
PERSONNAGE NON INCLUS
CONDOR FX
LE VRAI PROTOTYPE AIR-SOL
DU GROUP ACTION JOE
QUATRE VEHICULES E
Avec leur prototype top-se
réussissent les missions les p
MARK
CAPTAIN COSMOS
CONDOR
ACTION JOE
MILITAIRE
bazooka
2983
GENERATEUR D'

GROUP ACTION JOE
OPERATION CROIX ROUGE
TENTE AVEC TABLE ET SIEGE PLIANT
KIT A MONTER
CHENILLETTE TOUT TERRAIN
LA VERITABLE CHENILLETTE TOUT TERRAIN DU GROUP ACTION JOE
BOB Chasseur d'images
ELECTRIQUE
DANGER
CAPTAIN COSMOS
PERSONNAGES NON INCLUS
LE VEHICULE D'EXPLORATION PLANETAIRE D'ACTION JOE

BEFORE ACTION JOE
GI JOE & ACTION MAN
1964-1975

At the beginning there was GI Joe, the very first 12-inch action figure, the ancestor of Action Man, Action Joe and all the other action figures, which have existed for the past 40 years, for boys.

Before *GI Joe*, it was the little girls who had the privilege of playing with mannequin dolls since the appearance of Barbie in 1959.

The first principle was simple for *Hasbro*: to adapt the small, classic soldier to a mannequin doll like Barbie, but much more functional, with 21 articulations. Wooden models used by the designers inspired Don Levine, who was at the origin of this project. Applied for in 1963, the patent was registered in 1964, at the time of the launch of this new type of toy, which was neither a doll, nor a small soldier. Moreover, at that epoch Hasbro specified «*It isn't a doll, it's an action figure*». GI Joe, America's Movable Fighting Man was born.

GI JOE

The very first range of products rested on four action figures (Action Soldier, Action Sailor, Action Marine and Action Pilot) each incarnating an army corps of the United States (Army, Navy, Marine Corps and Air Force). Each action figure was supplied in an illustrated box presenting the hero in action, with a kit supplied separately. Gun, helmet, pack and other accessories were available apart. The boys had plenty to play 'at

In 1964 there were four figures: Action Pilot, Action Soldier, Action Marine and Action Sailor.

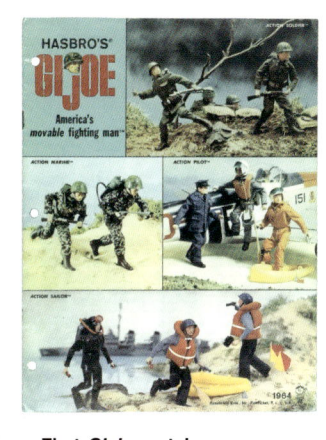

Above. First *GI Joe* catalogue of 1964

Opposite. *GI Joe* advertisement published in *Tintin* magazine in 1965.

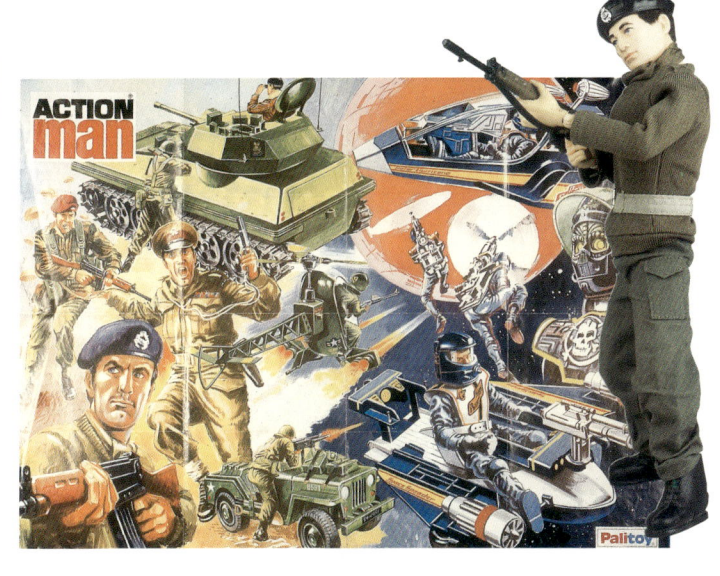

dolls', with subjects which couldn't have been manlier. At first, *GI Joe* was presented as being a miniature, based on real American soldiers, which was intended for boys and their father. The publicity photos presented a child of at least 12 years old, creating a giant diorama in 1/6 with the help of the '*good*' father, smoking the pipe. It was a game very like the electric train set with the slogan «*A new kind of fun… For Father and son!* » In his early days, *GI Joe* had painted, then, flock hair (a British invention), from 1967 he started to talk (Talking Joe), then continued his improvements until he had movable eyes and hands with flexible fingers.

To summarise *GI Joe* as a soldier would be ignoring the tremendous career of the ancestor of 12-inch action figures. With the Vietnam War, the military side conveyed by *GI Joe* was ill perceived. He was not the only toy to have suffered because of this situation. So, *Hasbro* decided to direct his range of products towards the Adventure. Sporting a beard, the hero explored wild countries in search of treasure, rare animals and strong sensations. From the Arctic to the hostile Jungle, Joe and his friends had great adventures. *Hasbro* adapted a large part of his military accessories, used elements of uniforms and repainted the vehicles. It was the beginning of the Adventure Team. Without losing the name he was given at birth, Joe now disposed of a second emblem, a red pastille stamped with an A and a T, interlaced. He also had a more muscular body (Muscle Body[1]) which reused this emblem from 1975 onwards.

ACTION MAN

From 1966, *GI Joe* made an observed entry in Great Britain under the name *Action Man* (and yes, it is the same!). His name was inspired by the television series 'Danger Man', who was very popular at this time. The toys were distributed (and often produced) by the firm Palitoy, under the *Hasbro* licence. Throughout the career of *Action Man*, *Palitoy* contributed a lot to the American firm. Thus, the flock hair giving a more realistic effect, the beard and the hands that could really hold objects were some of many improvements developed by the British for *Action Man*, which were later taken up by *Hasbro* for the original *GI Joe*. Contrary to *Hasbro*, *Palitoy* didn't change its direction and continued to commercialise the military figures, uniforms, jeeps and tanks alongside that of the Far-west, adventures, sporting and spatial. This earliest *Action Man* lasted longer than *GI Joe* since *Palitoy* only stopped his distribution [2] in 1984.

Before *Action Joe*, all the same, *GI Joe* toys imported from the USA were available in France from 1965 and more precisely in 1971. *Action Man* toys were also distributed in some shops from 1973 onwards.

In the USA, Hasbro had totally stopped *GI Joe's* career in 1978. The 12-inch action figure had just encountered a competitor of 'size' with the success of the 3 3/4" action figure from *Kenner* [3], but that didn't prevent foreign firms from continuing his commercialisation under licence, as was the case with *Céji Arbois* who distributed his version of *GI Joe: Action Joe*.

---

1. The Muscle Body was used for the majority of *Action Joe* figures between 1976 and 1981.
2. The production of *Action Man* was stopped by *Palitoy* in 1984, to be restarted in 1994 by *Hasbro* Europe and has been a tremendous success for more than ten years. For his part, *GI Joe* continued his career in the form of small action figures in the USA and in Europe and for the past six years in the form of the 12-inch figure again, but only in the USA.
3. See Special Series N° 1 of *Dixième Planète*.

ACTION JOE
THE SIX GLORIOUS 1976-1981

**After having been an imported toy, the action man for boys adopted a French identity.
His name was the fusion of GI Joe and Action Man.
He was named Action Joe.**

The Vietnam War tarnished the soldier image of *GI JOE* and *Action Man* and it was absolutely necessary, for *Céji*'s team, not to make a mistake where their position was concerned. *Action Joe* has been a turning point in the French toy industry in many people's eyes as much for the level of design, marketing and television advertising. *Action Joe* was also the element, which demonstrated that it was no longer possible to continue manufacturing everything in France. It was already the decline of part of the toy industry, like that of the textile industry, in France.

Genesis

The birth of *Action Joe* happened in two stages. The firm, which gave him life, was founded in 1969. The *Compagnie Générale du Jouet* (later best known under the name, *Céji*) was the regrouping of several toy manufacturers and distributors. Its origin goes back to the repurchasing of *Joustra* by a financial group of banks.

To carry out this operation, the bank of the European Union called on Mr. Philippe Mayer, who was at the time, president of the enterprise *Jouets Rationnels*. *Jouets Rationnels* was the principal importer and manufacturer of toys in France[1], to whom we notably owe the arrival of *Barbie* in 1963. It is also to Mr. Meyer that we owe the distribution in France of another great toy success: the Etch-a-Sketch.

The *Compagnie Générale du Jouet* included *Joustra*, *Clodrey* (who preceded *Corolle*[2]), *JEU* (*Jeux Educatifs Universels*), the soft toys *Lang* and *Arbois* and became the first European group in the Toy sector. Philippe Mayer was the deputy-managing director for research and development until 1975. During this period, *GI Joe* (in 1971) then *Action Man* (in 1973) was imported in France by *Céji*.

After having left the *Compagnie Générale du Jouet*, Mr. Meyer worked with *Hasbro*'s American head office. He was in charge of the organisation of production under the *Hasbro* licence for European countries [3], in close collaboration with Bill Lansing who was the Vice President of *Hasbro*. Ever since, Philippe Mayer has been a consultant with *Hasbro* France.

In 1976, his successor to the post of deputy managing director of *Céji Arbois*, in charge of Marketing, was Mr. Philippe L'Helgoualc'h who is the 'father' of *Action Joe*. It was Philippe L'Helgoualc'h, who worked on the reduction of import costs by negotiating directly with the factories based in Hong Kong and ordered the special productions for France under the *Hasbro* licence.

Mr. L'Helgoualc'h explains it himself: «*All that was vehicles and large parts had been made by the English and continued to be produced in England. On the other hand, all that was figures and clothes came from the same factory in Hong Kong. This factory, Cheung Hong Kong Industrial, was totally independent and produced many products for Hasbro. We tied up with this factory as it had the moulds for the figures and accessories and we tied up with the Hasbro factories in the United States and Palitoy in England to make all the large plastic parts and vehicles*».

It resulted in the production for the French market of a personalised range of products taken from the original moulds. This collection developed its own label which was devised after a brainstorming of which Philippe L'Helgoualc'h still remembers: «*We knew that it was GI Joe who was at the origin. There were historic reminiscences and we were going to attach ourselves to the history. Joe is an international name, pronounceable in all languages. Action because Action Man had already been here. This term was understandable in French. Action Joe, that was already good. I am not sure that to add Group to Action Joe was necessary, that came to complicate the logo*».

---

1. The *Jouets Rationnels* had such importance that this company published entire catalogues of toys in the pages of the big weeklies like *Paris Match* and *Jours de France*.
2. *Corolle* is a famous French brand of traditional dolls for little girls.
3. At that epoch, the firm *Hasbro* had no European bases. The American toy giant granted licences for the exploitation of its products abroad.

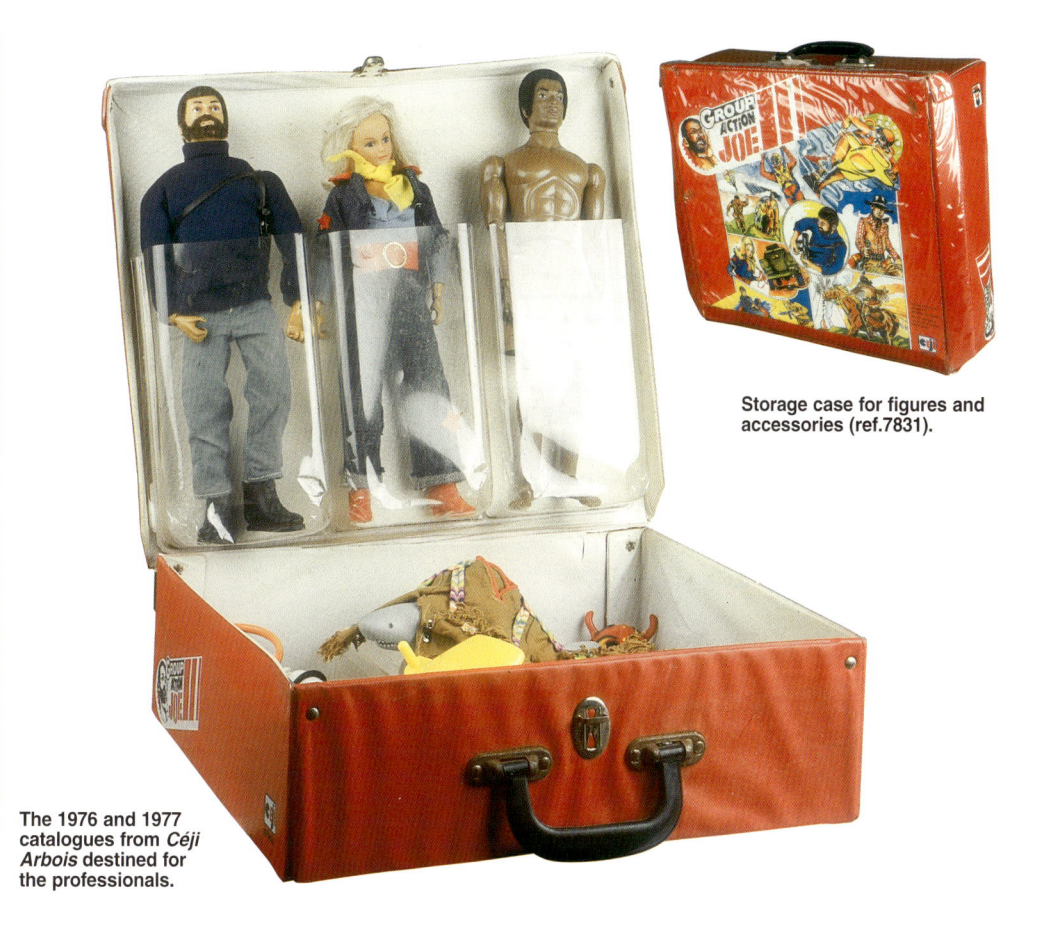

Storage case for figures and accessories (ref.7831).

The 1976 and 1977 catalogues from *Céji Arbois* destined for the professionals.

A EUROPEAN CO-PRODUCTION

Céji developed the *Action Joe* range of products in close collaboration with his European 'brothers' and particularly the Germans. Each developed its characteristics with distinct labels (see last chapter of this book). The former deputy-managing director of *Céji* recalls: «Germany, France, Italy and England tried to bring together their collection aware that each retained their own marketing. We all went to the same sources, trying to co-ordinate our quantities in terms of production and packaging, on the other hand, each was very different. In Germany it was the same thing. Between the France and Germany the packaging had roughly the same look, only the logo and the language changed. The whole thing worked due to the fact that we always succeeded in getting together in Hong Kong. We had three or four productivity campaigns. We had meetings over a five week period and went through the whole new collection from A to Z. We placed all our presales according to our respective countries. We produced films of all our packaging and all our booklets. It was exciting. We really worked as a team.

Our suppliers told us, that taken account of the all the quantities together, we could have enough series to produce such and such accessory (it would happen that we dropped an accessory in order to stay within the cost prices, which were in line with our objectives). The products left by boat throughout the year. At the end of the year, we brought in products for restocking by aeroplane. Even if that cost more, in the long run it allowed us to replenish supplies of missing products. We made a lower margin but we had a flexibility at the level of shop supplies». The Spanish have also been very active on *Céji*'s part.

For the principal toy firm in France it was not always obvious to de-localise in Asia or even in Europe. However, there were technical and economic necessities, which obliged the manager of *Céji* to juggle with the different options: «It became the 'lighthouse' collection for the Céji Group. That showed for the first time that it was important in the toy industry, not to seek to systematically manufacture everything by oneself. Our French toy group had factories in France and wished absolutely to make its factories profitable. I have succeeded in having cer-

The 76 and after 77 versions of the wooden canteen (ref.7593). It was sold empty in order to accommodate a figure and all its accessories.

tain plastic, injected products manufactured in the Joustra factories in Strasbourg. I had the Group factories functioning, but at the same time, I had that which could not be reasonably produced in France, manufactured externally. That's to say the small, plastic accessories, figures and outfits. For then it was necessary for me to have sufficient products produced in France or in the Common Market to be able, one day, to show the product on television.»

Joustra, although a group member, was in this case the sub-contractor of *Céji Arbois* for the *Action Joe* vehicles. Also the collection, which was coherent in the catalogues and toy shelves, was composed of toys from several origins. That's what permitted *Céji* to show the *Action Joe* toys in publicity spots on television. At that epoch, before broadcasting publicity it was necessary to submit the files to a commission to prove that at least 75% of the product was produced in the Common Market. «*When we sold a special* coffret *with a vehicle or figure shown on the Tele, we had to prove that the figure didn't represent more than 25% of the toy.*» Another solution consisted of not using a figure made in Asia. That is why some *Action Joe* figures came from the *Palitoy* factories, which were in the Common Market.

THE KEYS OF SUCCESS

One of the *Action Joe* successes resided without doubt in the fact that the marketing and commercial team was particularly involved. Mr. L'Helgoualc'h says on this subject moreover: «*We had very little means and we were enthusiasts. It was the enthusiasm of a fabulous team. It proved to be a great pleasure and we amused ourselves like fools.*» *Action Joe* wasn't just a reference in a catalogue. The members of the commercial department spoke of him like he was their child, it was a range which touched them and still today the «old boys» from *Céji Arbois* show a vast enthusiasm in recalling these years.

We studied each toy to be certain that it would please the public. For that there were of course lots of trials amongst children. But the best way of knowing the consumers' taste was to be in direct touch with the points of sale. The supremacy of the big superstores was not yet omnipresent and during the first years of the life of *Action Joe* it was possible to find these action men in toyshops only. Shops, which were supplied directly by *Céji* and not by, intermediate wholesalers. The objective of *Céji* was not to flood the market by trying to sell large quantities, which would have inevitably led to unsold goods at the retailers. «*There were very few products cancelled and very little overstocking because it was on-the-ground marketing with the retailers. When one controls the distribution with specialists, it is enough to go to see them to know the feedback of what the customers want (...) We had very few goods returned*» explained Philippe L'Helgoualc'h.

Opposite.
The Dune Cruiser from *Joustra*, which is at the origin of motorised vehicles for the *Group Action Joe*, was made in Strasbourg.

Below.
Example of a window display presented on the back of the 1977 catalogue for toy retailers.

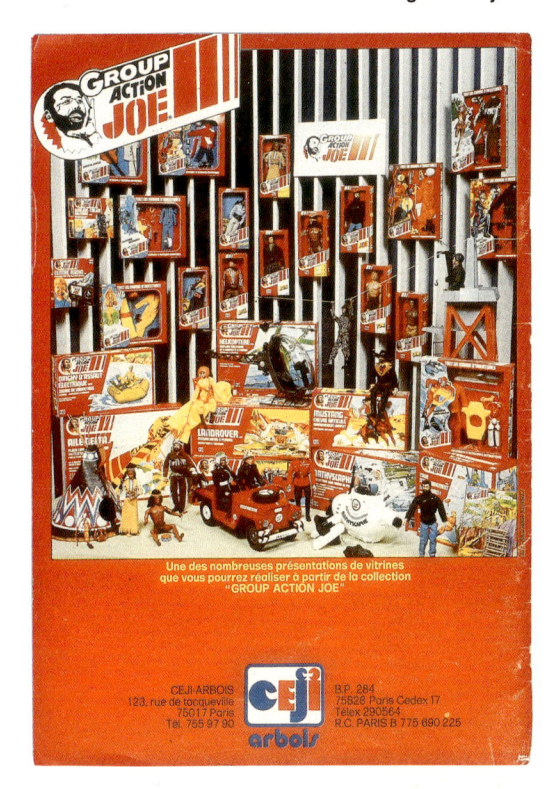

Shop window competitions were organised to implicate the professionals still some more in the *Action Joe* cause. The shops received a window display pack [4] in accordance with their order. The *Céji* representatives were trained to help the professionals. Then they passed by to take photos of the decorations. A committee was formed with professionals and consumers to designate the winners. The winning retailers gained a trip to the Far East to visit the factories. That permitted us to have shop windows showing the *Action Joe* toys to the advantage throughout the year.

Enormous, animated shop windows were completed in the large stores like the *Galeries Lafayette* at Christmastime.

The action figures were modified to be animated like robots in the sumptuous settings (like the great North with sledge dogs on the surface of the ice floes and frogmen below).

All the retailers also disposed of efficient promotion aids with mini-catalogues destined for the public, in parcels of 100 (ref. 4474), booklets to collect the cut-out stars from the boxes, supplied in packets of 50 (ref. 3550).

From 1977 onwards, the catalogues were produced under the control of *Céji*. More than one collector remembers not without emotion, the superb productions ornamenting these catalogues which made them dream. With the broadcasting of the television commercials and, faced with success, *Céji* found himself obliged to render the *Action Joe* collection available to wholesalers and the big chain stores. Paradoxically, it is from this moment that the toy sales are going to begin to suffer.

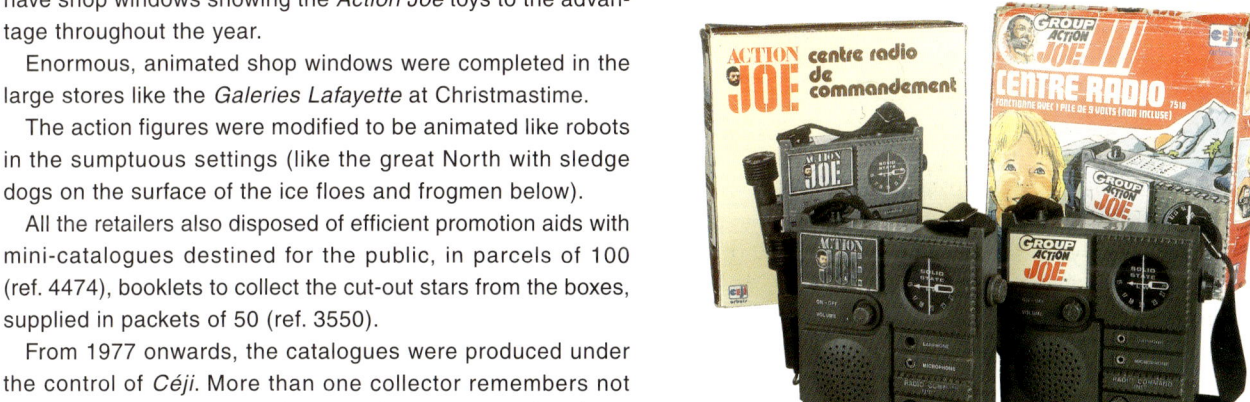

The Radio Centre was a real radio with a microphone. Here the 1976 version and the 1977 version.

4. There were some packs supplied with the window display like the pack " Fire Rescue " (ref. 4439) or ' Adventure in the West' (ref. 4438) proposed to retailers in 1976.

1976 THE BIRTH

In the first year, the logo was influenced by that of *GI Joe*. At that moment, the *Group Action Joe* was a sort of mixture between the British *Action Man* range by Palitoy and the last few years of the *GI Joe Adventure Team* which disappeared in the USA at the same epoch. Just like in the USA, the French toys were destined for children between 7 and 14. In our days, the modern *Action Man* figures are produced for the children of 4 years upwards.

From the start, the 1976 range consisted of six unnamed characters. There was the adventurer, the soldier, the cowboy, the Indian, the brown, bearded man in shorts and the black man in shorts. The photos illustrating the first catalogue for the general public and certain boxes (like the Assault Dinghy) are the clichés supplied with the licence that we find abroad in the *Action Man* or *Geyperman* (for Spain) catalogues. The small Comic books, which came with certain sets, were still in English and stamped with the *GI Joe* emblem. At the end of 76, the first woman arrived, she was entitled to a name: Jane.

1977 FIRST MAJOR CHANGES

The *Group Action Joe* acquired its own identity with a completely new look for the logo.

On it we see the outline of Joe, raising his left hand by way of a loudhailer as if to call his friends, shouting the name of the collection. Mr.L'Helgoualc'h recalls: « *The red bars, which were often used at that time notably in the Air France logo then in that of the TGV, made like an echo which loses itself in the long grass. It was very powerful. We did that with our publicity agent and Ghyslaine Fizet* [5].» The colour red, which was already the basic colour of the first '76 packaging, predominated totally from there on. The classic illustrations were replaced, a few at a time, by original designs with bright colours making one think of the comic style.

Another innovation, Joe lost his 'soldier' part to turn more towards the adventure. «*We very quickly realised that on the one hand it was necessary to make a soldier, but that the soldier must be integrated in a more global adventure by way of the adventures crossing the sand, the water, space and the Far-west. Which gave us much less military, more traditional and more open bases. We were aware that the soldiers inevitably aroused the critics.*

There were always the detractors of the military, but at the limit, the more the soldier was attacked the more he would sell. However, it was normal that taking account of the character and his new campaign, the adventure would continue independently from the soldier. That we did much more than the English. We did it, above all, with the Germans and the Italians.»

The characters were baptised and commenced to have movable eyes [6]. It was the bearded, brown figure (equipped from now on with eagle eyes) who became the team leader and carried the name of Joe. Two other girls rejoined the group, they were Peggy and Daïna. Thus, numerous sets were added to the catalogue. Also, the aspect of an out-door toy was put forward with the different presentations of accessories and vehicles. *Action Joe* could have a thousand adventures in the garden.

In 76, what was a trial shot became a master stroke which transformed into a phenomenon with a advertising campaign occupying two full pages in the children's press permitting them to discover the team of nine adventurers. Coloured display packs of the heroes, headed with the new logo were supplied to the shops. The accent is put on the adventure with slogans like «*More the toy is real, more the adventure is real*» or «*To create a whole world of adventures*».

From left to right.
The catalogues for the general public: 1976, 1977, 1978 (exists in two editions), 1979 (opens out as a poster), 1980 and 1981.

---

5. Ghyslaine Fizet who was in charge of marketing at *Céji*. She has been of precious help in the realisation of this book.
6. The pages which follow, detail the total collection of *Action Joe* with figures (*Comrades in adventure*), then the four principal themes (*A whole world of Adventures*), the technical details and the promotion. At the end of the book, you will find the totality of *Action Joe* products, which were commercialised by *Céji Arbois* between 1976 and 1981.

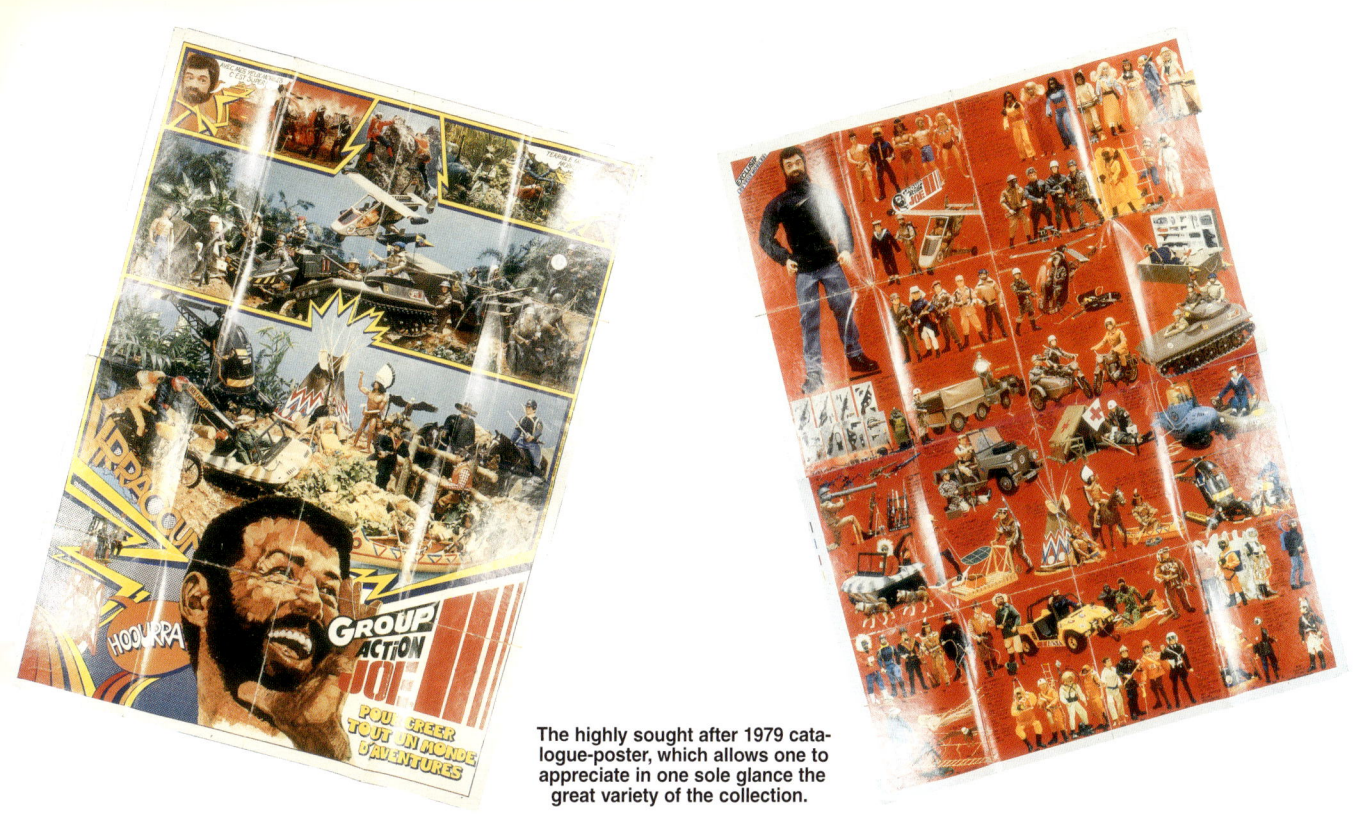

The highly sought after 1979 catalogue-poster, which allows one to appreciate in one sole glance the great variety of the collection.

1978 Progression

The *Group Action Joe* developed its peculiarities in creating a version of Jane with movable eyes and a Rahan under licence. From now on Bob was entitled to movable eyes whilst Sam, the black figure and Bill the cowboy disappeared. *Joustra*, being part of *Céji Arbois'* group, brought its contribution with a motorised all-purpose vehicle. *Action Joe* experienced his hours of glory in the publicity spots on the Tele.

1979 The Summit

The range reached its Zenith and counted for a very important number of references with new vehicles like the Capture Copter, the small all-purpose tracked vehicle and the campaign trailer, which only lasted for one year. The first, new-generation action figure from Palitoy joined the group as the character of Pilot Sam.

1980 In the Stars

Outer space was the fashion. *Goldorak* (*Grendizer*), *Albator* (*Captain Harlock*), the *Battle of the Planets* and many other series had been developed as by-products by *Céji Arbois* under licence. A « Bob » with movable eyes (Eagle Eyes) and having the same *Action Man* body as Sam made his appearance, under the name of Mark alias Captain Cosmos. Around him a spatial range of products was exploited with electric accessories and a Space Pirate set. A new *Joustra* vehicle came to complete the spatial adventure with a space tank decorated like the toys from the *Battle of the Planets*.

Other novelty in the packaging: the boxes with windows gave way to closed boxes presenting the photo of the action figure. It was the case for Captain Cosmos and Bob the Cameraman, a version distributed uniquely in France.

1981 The last year

The agreement between *Céji Arbois* and *Hasbro* finished at the end of 1981. This last year was marked by a new modification of the packaging. Photos replaced the designs, the orange-yellow colour predominated. One sensed that the range was running out of breath. It must be said that the *Action Joe* figures were the same as those of *GI Joe*, which hadn't been produced for several years already. In the USA, *Hasbro* got ready to enter *G I Joe* into a new era. The by-products from *Star Wars* had done a lot of harm to the action man for boys, the small, all-plastic action figure was the fashion. In the USA, *GI Joe* was going to come back in the form of 3 3/4"(10cm) figures accompanied by a multitude of vehicles mixing military and science fiction characteristics. In France, *Céji Arbois* got ready to turn the page with sales promotions reuniting the figure with the set or the figure with a vehicle.

Action Joe left the place for *Action Man* in 1982 which was be distributed by *Miro-Meccano* (see chapter After *Action Joe*). *Céji Arbois* disappeared some time later.

After six years of adventures, Joe and his companions have left an undying memory in the minds of a whole generation. In our days, these children now grown-ups, are happy to rediscover this hero in their trunk or in the specialist shops for toys of collection.

COMRADES IN ADVENTURE

The *Group Action Joe* was made up of adventurers, men and women who formed the basis of the toy collection. With the passing of time, some have left the *Group* whilst others have joined it. There have also been heroes from comics and TV series who came very to Joe and his team.

In 1976, the very first *Action Joe* figures don't have names[1]. They were six in number. Each was described by their function: 'the soldier', 'the adventurer', 'the cowboy', 'bearded figure in short' etc… It was more a question of the basic figures designated by the generic term, *Action Joe* than of real, engaging comrades. Two of the figures only wear shorts as a way of being 'entry' products for the range, which make necessary the additional purchase of a set.

Nothing indicated who was the team leader. Moreover, the first advertisements put the brown, bearded figure in the spotlight and paradoxically, the first logo carried the blond, bearded figure's head.

Top. **Special promotion stickers of 1977.**
Below left. **Bob and Jane in their 1978 packaging.**

In 1977, the figures are going to become characters recognisable by their Anglo-Saxon names. In fact, that will begin at the end of '76 with the arrival of the first girl, baptised Jane. « t seemed important to us to give names to these characters so that the children could communicate with them. We needed to move away from the generic term of figure to a band of adventurers. It is in 1977 that we invented a notion of a team to create a whole world of adventures and it is then that we give them all names. It was extremely funny to do. We hoped for a dreamlike affinity. Whence names which weren't necessarily French names» explains Phillipe L'Helgoualc'h. The bearded brown figure will quickly become the leader of the team and bears the name of Joe[2], he will have movable eyes (Eagle Eyes) and will wear the costume which was dedicated to the Adventurer in 1976. Many copies arrived on the market. The name also permitted us to doubly protect the concept.

Several figures under licence (*Rahan*, *Albator*, *Zorro*) were developed by *Céji Arbois*, whilst other projects didn't see the light of day, like the diver from the crew of Commander Cousteau[3].

---

1. As was the case for the *GI Joes* and the majority of *Action Man*.
2. The beard appeared on *GI Joe* when the adventure side took precedence over the soldier side due to the Vietnam war. In 1976, *Céji* was inspired by the American publicity images, the most recent of the epoch, to define the characters. After that, the direction taken by the French was totally independent.
3. Commander Cousteau refused this project, which must be done under licence.

The soldier (ref. 2953) and the adventurer (ref. 2952) of 1976.

Joe

Joe, more commonly called *Action Joe* (ref. 7945) is the leader of the team. It is only at the beginning of the second year of existence of the *Céji Arbois* range that he will appear. His function is centred on the adventure. With his thick mariner's sweater, his beard and his movable eyes (Eagle Eyes), he is the best known of all the *Group Action Joe* figures. The logo, revamped in 1977, gives him stardom and he will be shown on the first page of all the catalogues. His outfit was worn, in 1976, by the blond, bearded adventurer (ref. 2952). The latter was not yet called Tom.

In 1976, there was a brown, bearded figure sold in shorts (ref.7566) and whose eyes were not yet movable.

Tom

This bearded blond had begun a fine career since he strongly risked becoming the leader of the team. In 1976, he wore the costume composed of a blue pullover, jeans walking boots and a black holster with a revolver. As an adventurer, he bore the reference 2952. In 1977, when Joe made his appearance, the bearded blond will become Tom and at this moment, will not wear more than plain shorts (ref. 7566), taking the place of the brown, bearded figure of '76. In 1981 Tom will lose his name to become one of the two Invincibles (ref. 4466).

Bob

Bob started his career in the *Group Action Joe* under the designation 'soldier' (ref.2953) in 1976. The following year, he is going to receive his name and will keep his soldier's outfit and the same catalogue reference. Bob, in soldier version, is the *Action Joe* figure who is the closest thing to the original *GI Joe*.

In 1978, he will be endowed with the movable eyes mechanism and will change his look and function. Dressed in plain beige shorts (ref. 2655), Bob will become, in his turn, an entry product of the range. For all that, his soldier's uniform didn't disappear from the collection and will become the French Soldier Set. Two years later, he will wear khaki overalls and walking boots. Still endowed with Eagle Eyes, he will keep his catalogue reference until the end of 1980. He won't be present in the 1981 collection, supplanted by another Bob: Bob the Cameraman.

Bob the Cameraman

Bob the Cameraman (ref. 7930) is a very special figure, since he was only developed for the French market. Appearing in 1980, he was sold in a closed box. His body corresponds to that of the Indian, Œil de Lynx (Eye of the Lynx), but he has blue, movable eyes. This peculiarity makes him a rare toy and even a legend, since some collectors think that

Œil de Lynx (ref. 7946) and Joe (ref.7945) of 1977.

Bearded brown (ref. 7566) of 1976 and Sam (ref. 2999) of 76/77.

4. For all that, he really existed since two Bob Cameramen of that epoch have been used in the realisation of this book.

re of the Gorilla set. His function was clear, he was a cameraman reporting on animals in exotic countries.

TED

Bob disappeared from the 1981 collection but his face with movable eyes was that of a newcomer, Ted (ref. 7951). A soldier, whose outfit was a simplified, parachutist uniform of the Red Berets.

BILL THE COWBOY

The cowboy figure (ref. 7597) is another speciality for the French market. It was possible to buy a set to dress any Group member as a cowboy and at the same time, one could buy the figure already dressed (but without the camp accessories). This figure is strictly identical to that which was named Bob. In 1977, the cowboy will receive the name of Bill. However, in 1978, with the arrival of movable eyes for Bob, Bill disappeared from the catalogue. This name will remain connected to the set.

THE INDIANS

He, who says cowboy, says Indian. The first year, just like for the future Bill, the Indian (ref. 7598) was in fact a figure of the 'Bob type', dressed in the set (ref. 7568).

The following year, this Indian had disappeared from the collection to leave the place for Œil de Lynx (Eye of the Lynx ref. 7946) who was, with Joe, endowed with the first movable eyes (Eagle Eyes). His eyes were black and his skin was bronzed to look more like a 'Redskin'. His long-haired wig was stuck on his cranium

The two versions of Tom (ref. 7566) with green shorts (77) and blue shorts (79).

he has never existed[4]. He was dressed in the same khaki overalls as the 1980 Bob, wearing a hat borrowed from the Soldier of the Tropics set (just like the machete) and a camera from the Captu-

Bob Eagle Eyes (ref. 2655) in shorts (1978) and in overalls (1980).

Ted (ref. 7951) of 1981.

Bob, cameraman (ref. 7930) of 1980.

The cowboy (ref. 7597) of 76, who becomes Bill in 77.

The Indian (ref. 7598) of 1976.

without any flock hair. Eye of the Lynx was developed for France and Germany at the same time. His career was brief since it only stretched from 1978 to 1980. His body will serve as the base for the cameraman, Bob.

SAM

Sam is a name, which designated numerous characters. That began in 1977 with the black figure in shorts (ref. 2999) which had appeared in 1976. He disappeared from the '78 collection. In 1979, another Sam made his appearance. It concerned a blond with Eagle Eyes, whose body was totally redesigned. The pilot Sam (ref. 4012) was an *Action Man* equipped with a new body. His body is stamped with the British logo just like his orange helmet. In 1980, Sam will become a motorcyclist (ref. 7978), then in 1981, a diver (ref. 7950). Sam's frogman's suit existed in two colours (orange and black) under the same catalogue reference.

CAPTAIN COSMOS

In 1980, the figure Mark Captain Cosmos (ref. 7979) was the hero of the very new space collection. This Space Ranger owes his costume to *Action Man*, who also had a similar collection at the same epoch. His body was, just like that of Pilot Sam, a Palitoy original and his hair is brown. The base of Captain Cosmos's laser gun comes from the harpoon gun in the Diver's set for girls. In 1981, Captain Cosmos experienced a colour variant concerning his doublet with the yellow edging changed to red.

The pilot, Sam (ref. 4012) of 1979.

Sam, diver (ref. 7950) of 1981.

Sam, motorcyclist (ref. 7978) of 1980.

Mark Captain Cosmos (ref. 7979) of 1980.

The Anonymous

Beyond 1977, other figures were commercialised in the Action Joe collection without however, having a name. Also in 1978, the two *coffrets* contained a Palitoy figure with an older body than those of other Group members. A bearded, brown figure with painted eyes was supplied with the Radio Communications Centre (ref. 3512) and a brown, beardless figure with Eagle Eyes was supplied with the all terrain vehicle (ref. 2724), like the Power Hog from *Palitoy*. In 1981, two naked figures were sold under the label, The Invincibles. It concerned a brown figure with painted eyes (ref. 7983) corresponding to Bob and Bill before 1978 and of Tom, renamed (ref. 4466).

Rahan

Rahan (ref. 2656) was the first character under licence integrated in the *Group Action Joe*. Rahan, the son from the savage ages was a celebrated hero of French comics in the children's magazine *Pif Gadget*. He's a character in the Tarzan style. These adventures take place in prehistoric times. Rahan is entitled to the production of a special head, with real long, hair, mounted on a basic body and to the invention of specific accessories. Accessories that one could find in a blister pack (ref. 2682). Rahan was part of the collection from 1978 to 1979. This toy could be associated with some of the accessories from the adventure world, like the hammock, the bridge made from liana, or the crocodile.

Albator

Second 12-inch figure under licence. Albator was commercialised in 1979 but wasn't part of the *Action Joe* collection. Albator, the Captain privateer is the French name for Captain Harlock, a celebrated hero of the Japanese cartoon. His head and his set have been created for the occasion, for the rest, they are indeed elements from *Action Joe*. The figure's body is under the *Hasbro* licence. He wears the same boots as those from the Fireman, the German Soldier or the State Police sets. The small pistol is found in the 1980 Space Pirate set, as is the skull and crossbones logo. The reference 1371 of this figure doesn't correspond to the references designating *Action Joe* toys.

Zorro

The figure of the masked avenger, Zorro (ref. 7973), just like the 1978 set of the same name and that of Davy Crockett in '77, will be made the object of a *Disney* licence in 1981. As for the figure, it will not have any modification and it is a standard head with movable eyes that will be hidden under Zorro's mask.

Action Joe in the feminine!

France is one of the rare countries to have developed girl figures under the *Hasbro* licence in the period '76-'81. *Céji* developed three characters, Jane, Peggy and Daïna.

The figure supplied with the Radio Communication Centre (ref. 3512).

The figure supplied with the all terrain vehicle (ref. 2724).

The Invincibles of 1981: bearded blond (ref. 4466) and brown (ref. 7983).

The blond Jane (ref. 7867) made her first appearance at the end of '76 in the catalogues for the general public. It is interesting to note that according to the photos in this catalogue, it concerned a prototype of a female body and not a definitive figure. The hands are outstretched and the elbows are not jointed. The version that was commercialised had prehensile hands and standard articulations for all the *Group Action Joe* girls.

In 1977 Jane, always dressed in jeans that were very fashionable at that epoch, was entitled to a new packaging (ref. 7905). The squaw, Daïna (ref. 7947) and the adventurer, Peggy (ref. 7904), joined her. At this moment, the commercial brochures subtitle '*for girls and boys of 6 to 14 years*'. The managers from *Céji* noticed that lots of girls play with their brother and that they appreciated *Action Joe*, notably in the framework of adventure games. It was an attempt to broaden the concept. However, if Jane (whose name was an echo of Joe) was a strong concept, the other female characters don't seem to have had the same impact. In 1978, *Céji* brings the amelioration of movable eyes to Jane (ref. 2657). Then, she is going to change outfit as do her two friends.

They wear coloured dungarees with a belt and rediscover bare feet. They always have their golden Colt. In 1980 Jane and Peggy disappear from the range, only Daïna will stay in the collection. She will disappear from the catalogue the following year.

Albator (ref. 1371) was not part of the *Group Action Joe*. For all that, this 1979 toy is of the same production.

Rahan (ref. 2656) and the blister pack of his accessories (ref. 2682) under licence, *Pif Gadget* dating from 1978.

Zorro (ref. 7973) under *Disney* licence of 1981.

Jane (ref. 7867 in 1976 and ref. 7905 in 1977)

Daïna (ref. 7947) dates from 1977.

Peggy (ref. 7904) dates from 1977. Photo from french catalogue.

Jane eagle eyes (ref. 2657) of 1978.

avec un pistolet d'or

Daïna (ref. 7947) in her 1978 version.

Peggy (ref. 7904) in her 1978 version.

23

24

25

A WHOLE WORLD OF ADVENTURES

The great strength of the *Group Action Joe* resided in the variety of adventures in which Joe and his comrades could be 'brought to life'. One single figure could, with the addition of accessories or a change of outfit, be transformed into soldier, adventurer, lifesaver, cowboy or hero of space opera.

Four fields of activity form the *Group Action Joe*'s adventure world, which are detailed in the following pages. First of all, there are the military campaigns, which are historically at the origin of the birth of *GI Joe* and *Action Man*. In the broad sense, the adventure of the exploration of exotic places, like the depths of the ocean, the jungle or the Polar Regions is an important component of the success of *Action Joe* in France. From 1977 onwards the Far West became a field that he had all to himself, with numerous products. Finally, the space adventures arrived late in the day one year before the disappearance of *Group Action Joe*.

A COHERENT RANGE OF PRODUCTS

Figures, blister packs, sets and vehicles formed a collection with modules, allowing parents to regularly offer their children elements to help them to use their imagination. Every year, new references[1] came to complete or sometimes replace those, which in our days constitute a legendary collection.

The total compatibility between the different elements of the game did not in any way, enclose the child in a single field. At any moment, his imagination could permit him to mix places, epochs and functions to create his own adventures. The first sets existed in two forms, either in a cardboard *coffret* or in a blister pack. In the case of the blister packs, two cards allowed one to reunite the clothes and the accessories of one set. Also for example, to create A Russian soldier there was the solution of dressing a Bob with the uniform and accessories set (ref. 7569) or with the uniform in a blister pack (ref. 7579) accompanied or not, with his accessories (ref. 7580). Later, sets were equally separated in blister packs like the In the open sky outfit that was available in a set (ref. 7868) from the end of 76, then also in two blister packs reuniting the parachute (ref. 7934) and the clothes (ref. 7933) from 1977 onwards. It was also possible to mix clothes for a figure by reuniting blister packs that weren't necessarily connected.

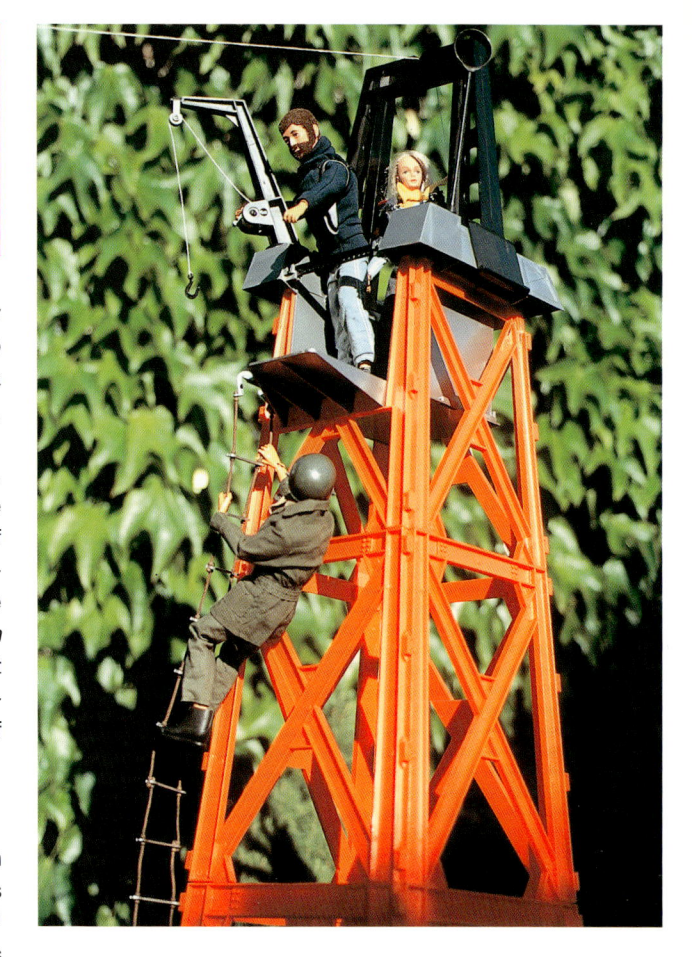

In 1978, information booklets were added to some sets. Thus allowing children to play intelligently by learning the rudiments of karate or to know more about a fireman's job.

The vehicles were relatively onerous toys, which weren't within the reach of everyone's pocket. Their presence in the catalogue and shop windows sometimes just made one dream. Fortunately, accessories like the parachute landing container (ref. 7080) or the inflatable boat (ref.7913) were the veritable stopgaps.

---

1. See Index (pages 80-82), which lists all the *Action Joe* toys from 1976 to 1980, classed by category (figures, sets, vehicles etc.)

Left page.
The training tower (ref. 7830 and 7903). The parachute landing container (ref. 7080) which was sold such as it was in a window display pack of 24 parts. The accessories were inside it.

Left.
Sam gets ready to descend the tower.

Below.
The numerous weapons sold in blister packs. Photo from the 1980 catalogue.

Opposite.
Contents details of a box from that epoch with toy, the sheet of stickers and the instructions. It concerns the small all-purpose tracked vehicle (ref. 4033) of 1979.

Below.
The camp bed (ref. 2794) was associated for a long time with the hospital.

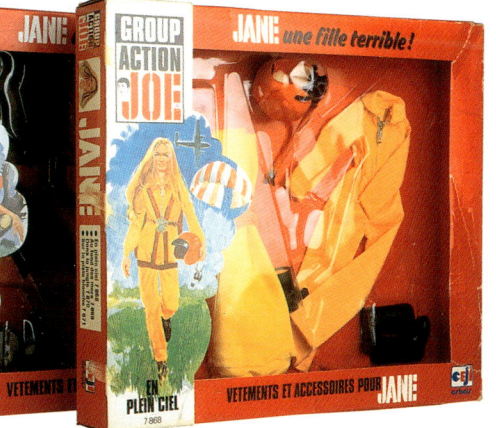

Various blister packs and sets

The Morse lamp (ref. 7572) was produced in blister pack from 1976 to 1978.

27

MILITARY

Initially, *GI Joe* was the adaptation of the traditional tin soldiers in the form of a 'doll for boys' better known as an action figure. During his career he personified the different armies of the United States then he also wore the uniforms of other countries. The choice of uniforms was particularly orientated towards the Second World War. In their turn, the British developed a large range of soldiers with sets never produced in the USA. So it was entirely natural that in its turn *Group Action Joe* be influenced by this tendency. If certain uniforms, like that of the Japanese soldier were not reproduced in the French range, we find the German, the Russian and the Australian soldiers and the French Resistance Fighter.

THE EQUIPMENT SETS

Since 1976, the principal uniforms accompanied by their specific accessories have been defined. The American, German, English, Russian and tropical (in fact Australian) soldiers have been commercialised as from the launch of the *Group Action Joe*. Since then, few changes have intervened. The Officers' sets (English, French and German) were withdrawn from the catalogue at the end of 1976. The figure, Bob wore fatigue dress and a helmet until 1978. At this date his outfit became the French soldier's set (ref. 2670). The innovations came in 1979 with the arrival of the Tank commander, the motorbike dispatch rider and the Africa Korps. In 1980, new uniforms came to reinforce the ranks with the American para (6 June 44), the Israeli soldier (with an Uzi), the German para and a Saharan commando.

American Parachutist equipment set dating from 1980.

THE VEHICLES

Absent from the initial American *GI Joe* range, the Land Rover is one of the numerous contributions from the *Action Man* range. Its 'so British' right-hand-drive was reversed from 1977 with a model developed by *Geyper* for Europe. Some accessories were available to complete the Land Rover. There was a four-wheeled trailer. This toy was only commercialised in 1979 under the reference 4043. A cover destined to complete it was sold separately (blister pack ref. 4047). The light, 105 mm canon could also be towed by the Land Rover. This model very close to the reality could genuinely fire shells. The cartridge cases have to be withdrawn before re-arming. Inspired by the anti aircraft defence searchlights, the army exercise searchlight uses batteries as with a torchlight. The switch, well positioned in the back of the lamp, allows one to use it in Morse code or in continuous mode. It can be installed at the back of the Land Rover or in the campaign trailer. The Land Rover will

The special operations kit contained a radio, grenades, a spade, a knife, a sub-machine gun, a pair of boots, a stove, a pistol, a flask, a cup, a mess tin with cutlery, a pair of binoculars and an American type helmet. In 1976, he happened to find a British helmet, a little known variant. You can see on this photo the 1976 kit and the one, which was sold between 1977 and 1981.

The English Soldier's equipment set was also available in blister packs (uniform and accessories), it concerned a big classic that was distributed throughout the existence of *Action Joe*.

This very handsome set for the British Officer was only available in France in 1976. Photo taken from the 1976 french order catalogue.

The German Officer and the German Soldier. The officer equipment set was only distributed during 1976.

This electric machine gun accessory was hardly diffused and disappeared from *Céji*'s order catalogue as from the end of 1976.

The Bazooka n the first blister pack version dating from 1976. The mortar with its spring system, that can launch shells.

The second electric machine gun accessory (ref. 5601) disposed of a motor to draw the cartridge strip in order to obtain a better realism. The battery housing is found in the munitions case.

29

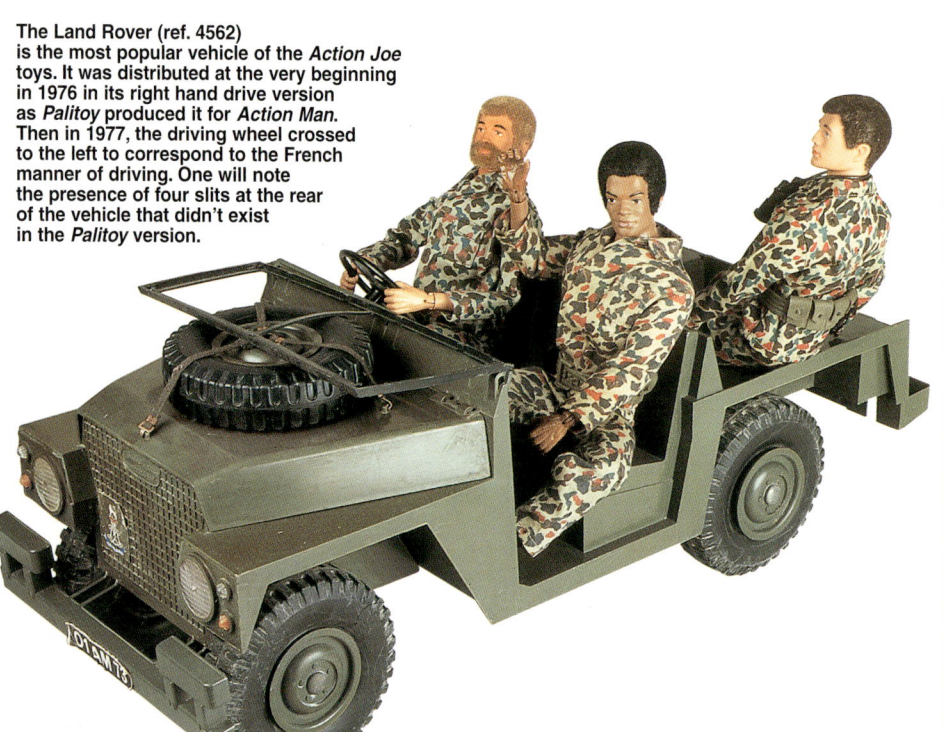

The Land Rover (ref. 4562) is the most popular vehicle of the *Action Joe* toys. It was distributed at the very beginning in 1976 in its right hand drive version as *Palitoy* produced it for *Action Man*. Then in 1977, the driving wheel crossed to the left to correspond to the French manner of driving. One will note the presence of four slits at the rear of the vehicle that didn't exist in the *Palitoy* version.

A convoy composed of two Land Rovers (one of which carries the searchlight) towing the light 105 mm canon and the campaign trailer (which was only available in 1979).

The 105 mm canon can really fire shells. The munitions are loaded in the same manner as for a real canon. This toy was only available in France between 1980 and 1981.

The all-purpose trapper vehicle is a strange, upright vehicle from Great Britain in 1979. On board, there are two *Action Joes* wearing variants of the commando parachutist Red Beret's uniforms (fabric beret and plastic beret).
In front of him, a Green Beret whose 1980 set corresponds to the French Paras uniform.

The searchlight for the army exercises really works. It is possible to use it to communicate in Morse code. It can be placed at the rear of the Land Rover and in the campaign trailer.

31

The helicopter, in its olive-green, military version only appeared in the *Group Action Joe* in 1977. In 1976 it was in the yellow, civilian version. It was possible to paint it in the Fireman or State Police versions with the *Humbrol* paints. Here you have a modified example with the camouflage version.

The Officer's tent with a member of the *Group* dressed as the 1976 French Officer opposite four *Action Joes* in French soldiers uniform dating from 1978.

The four-wheel drive Commando is the military version of the *Joustra Dune Cruiser*. It was adapted in 1980. It can take the electric machine gun. Joe, who descends from the four-wheel drive, wears the uniform of the Saharan Commando (set inspired by the SAS of 1942). Photo taken from the 1981 catalogue.

Below
The First Aid tent replaced the officer's tent in 1977, it was the same model with a Red Cross printed on each side. It was sold with a folding chair and a table. It completed the set 'Operation Red Cross' which existed since 1976.

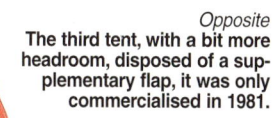

Opposite
The third tent, with a bit more headroom, disposed of a supplementary flap, it was only commercialised in 1981.

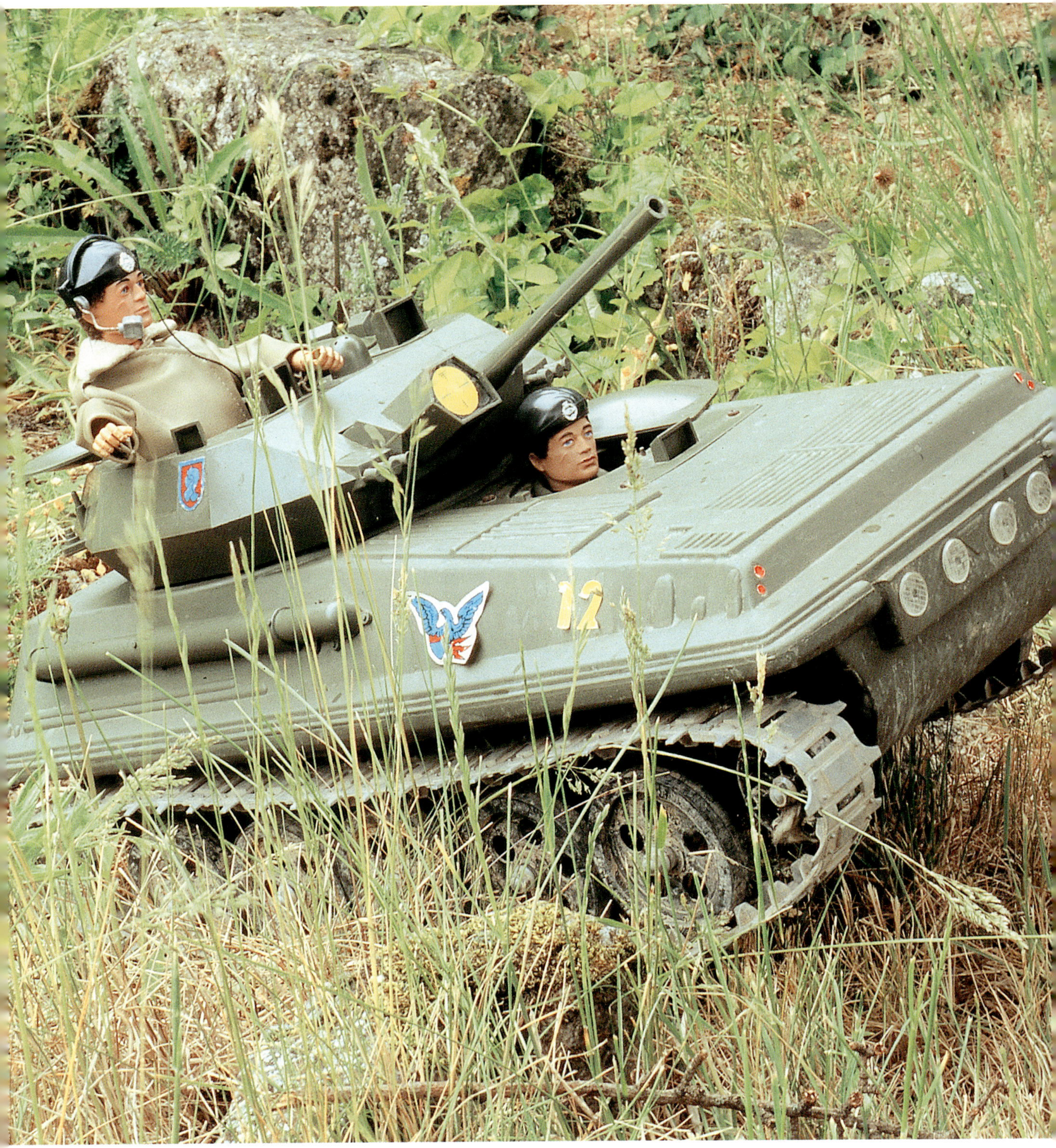
12

The celebrated soldier of the Foreign Legion (ref. 4544). In this photo, one can see the kepi that is found under the white fabric.

The modern American Soldier's set equipped with an M16 Assault Rifle is the most standard set with collectors.

The Marine Gunner set dating from 1978 (ref. 2673) is equally a French exclusive. The Israeli Soldier (ref. 7930) with his Uzi exclusive dating from 1980.

not be the only motor used by the *Group Action Joe* soldiers. The four-wheeled drive Commando joins it from 1980 onwards. It concerns the second adaptation of the *Joustra* Dune Cruiser. This French creation is truly motorised and can, like the 1978 Fighter, move around on its own. Little innovation: It can carry the electric machine gun. The helicopter is inspired by the Bell H-13H, it was commercialised in the yellow, civilian version in the USA. It was the same in France for the first year and it is in 1977 that *Céji* distributed the military version under the *Action Joe* label. The red version of the Paris firemen seen in the catalogues was, as was indicated, only possible after having repainted it with the special paint for models. It is the same thing for the State Police version.

**The Scorpion tank is modern armour of the British Army. It joins the *Group Action Joe* in 1978. It can hold three figures. It also can be painted in different ways as was indicated on its box.
The Tank Commander's set with its famous jacket dates from 1979.**

The small, light British Scorpion Tank appeared, of course, with *Action Man* in 1972, before rejoining the *Group Action Joe* in 1978. Its movable gun turret, its hatchways, its rotating canon and its tracks made it a very realistic vehicle. Its commercialisation will stop in France at the end of 1979. For quick and light movements, motorbikes have been provided in the *Group*. The motorbike and sidecar will make its entry in 1978, followed in 1979 by a small motorbike (in fact, the same motorbike without the sidecar). The sidecar is equipped with a machine gun and closely resembles that used by the German patrols.

THE TENTS

The military tents, three in number, are all conceived from the same model. The first in 1976, the Command tent was rapidly replaced by the First Aid tent the following year (which kept the same catalogue reference) to complete the Nurse's Set. A Red Cross printed on each

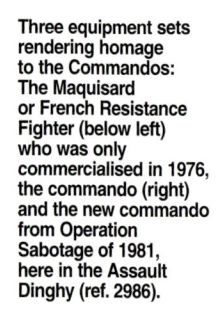

Above, from left to right.
German parachutist set (ref. 4041) from 1979. **Soldier in the Tropics set (ref. 5604)** from 1976. It was also available in two blister packs (ref. 7583 and 7584). **RAF, Royal Air Force Fighter Pilot set (ref. 7938)** dates from 1980.

Three equipment sets rendering homage to the Commandos: The Maquisard or French Resistance Fighter (below left) who was only commercialised in 1976, the commando (right) and the new commando from Operation Sabotage of 1981, here in the Assault Dinghy (ref. 2986).

side of the canvas is the only difference between them. This version was continued for several years before being replaced in 1981 by a more evolved model that included an awning.

SOLDIERS OF THE PEACE

In spite of this military appearance, the *Group Action Joe* did not put the notion of war in the forefront. One doesn't disclose any exacerbated patriotism either. There is no enemy opposing Joe and his men. With *Action Joe*, the soldiers from all countries and all epochs associated with each other for a common mission. A mission that was always centred on the adventure or humanitarian aid (like with the game competition 'Operation Niagara'). In the different catalogues one will often see the German soldier of 39-45 and a Russian soldier associated with an American soldier of the Vietnam epoch, or an Israeli soldier attached to a parachuting German.

The Alpine Fighter has known several versions between 1976 and 1981.

The 1979 Africa Korps set.

The motorbike (ref. 2742) and the sidecar (ref. 2715), driven by Tom in dispatch rider's uniform (ref. 4019). This set is quite rare as it was commercialised for one year only in 1979.

The American Machine Gunner who was commercialised from 1980 onwards.

The 1976 Russian Soldier.

37

ADVENTURE

In the minds of the managers of *Céji*, the adventure was the first aspect of *Group Action Joe*. At the launch of *Action Joe*, this field was for all that in the minority with only five sets (Leader of the Rope Party, Capture of the Gorilla, King of the Sky, In Deep Seas and Underwater Fisherman). Very quickly, from 1977 on, the adventure is going to outstrip the military environment with the slogan '*to create a whole world of adventures*'.

The Adventure with a capital 'A', regroups all that was contemporary at that epoch: the jungle, the depths of the sea, the exploration of the frozen North and the rescue operations. Climbing, the parachute jump and the espionage also, have completed this domain. I include the all-French sets, which are the Paris Fireman (appeared in 1977), the State Police motorcyclist (1977) and the Republican Guard (appeared in 1978). These last outfits are halfway between the soldiers and the adventure. But since in 1977, *Céji* developed a specific sales promotion around the Fire theme[1] at the time of the launch of the Fireman and Police sets and as it was still in the catalogues and the advertisements, it seemed logical to me to do as much in this book.

The first vehicles will be military (other than the '76 helicopter). As from 1977, it was advised to paint them in order to make them vehicles for emergencies or adventure. Afterwards, the exploration vehicles were specifically distributed as was the motorised Dune Cruiser from *Joustra*, which will join the *Group* in 1978 under the term Fighter.

ON LAND

The jungle is going to take a large place amongst the adventures of Joe and his team as the tropical forest introduces varied dangers. Several animals sold in blister packs will come to add spice to the explorations with, notably a crocodile (ref. 7921), a giant spider (ref. 7919) and two snakes (ref. 7920). The Capture of the gorilla (ref. 7123) introduced the first dangerous animal from 1976 on. It concerned a pygmy gorilla, which Joe must capture with the aid of a net. A small flat-bottomed boat was supplied with the outfit. It was a best seller, which was produced without interruption, by *Céji* from 1976 until the end of *Action Joe*. One of the four sets for Jane, commercialised at the end of 76 will be consecrated to the jungle (ref. 7870). The following year, a Safari outfit with a large hat came to complete this line. The Radio Communication Centre coffret, which contained a figure also, dressed in the Safari outfit[2] appeared at the end of 1977. The action figure, Bob the Cameraman and his Jeep will complete this domain, which was adorned with original accessories like the hammock and the bridge made from liana.

---

1. It is noted that the Red Cross Intervention set (ref. 7595) was also associated with the fire theme.
2. But without the hat which was drawn on the cardboard scene.

Above.
The Capture of the Gorilla coffret comprised of a boat, a pygmy gorilla, a canteen, a net, a gun with telescopic lens, a video camera and a camouflage outfit without shoes.

Left page.
Leader of the Rope Party is one of the very first equipment sets of 1976. The crocodile, animal sold alone in blister pack (ref. 7921) from 1977.

Opposite
The Liana Bridge (ref. 7924) was sold on a card. Not very easy to use, it allowed one to stretch a real liana bridge between tree branches to get the *Group* members, who didn't suffer from vertigo, across!

Below
Girl in the Jungle equipment set (ref. 7870), Safari equipment set for man (ref. 7907) and jungle outfit for girl in blister pack without accessories.

39

Opposite
The Radio Communication Centre (ref. 3512) was a coffret comprised of a cardboard scene, representing a hut in the middle of vegetation and monkeys, a radio and its bearded operator.
The radio disposed of a light, which permitted the use of the Morse code, a luminous radar screen and a sound function to listen to Joe's 'radio messages'. In fact, these messages are recorded on discs. A system devised for the talking figures is mounted in the radio centre in order to defile the messages one after the other by pressing a key.

Below
The Condor FX-01 is an aeroplane made up of modules. Its rotating wings permit a vertical take-off. It was supplied with removable floats to transform it into a seaplane. It also has a hold, which can contain the accessories.

40

The military Land Rover painted in a Safari version.

The outfit 'In the open sky' (ref. 7868).

The Fighter, a motorised, battery-powered vehicle created by *Joustra*. One can also see the giant spider. Photo extracted from the 1978 catalogue.

Below left.
The Capture Copter, modernised version of the helicopter, disposed of floats and a grabber at the front. A protective grill had replaced its canopy. It was only commercialised during 1979 under the reference 4046. This second helicopter was a predisposed tool of the very new pilot, Sam.

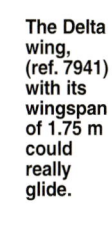

The Delta wing, (ref. 7941) with its wingspan of 1.75 m could really glide.

The 'King of the Sky' set for men was only available in the deluxe coffret version (ref. 2989).

The classic helicopter in its yellow livery, uniquely in 1976.

41

The all terrain vehicle (ref. 2724) was sold with its driver with Eagle Eyes, in tropical outfit.

IN THE DEPTHS OF THE SEA

Underwater exploration has always been a big success. Since 1976 there was the underwater fisherman in an orange wet suit, the diving suit for men and the blue divers outfit for Jane. Later in 1981, a black wet suit has also appeared in the collection. There exists a colour difference in the air bottles of the underwater fisherman, which were white in the set (ref. 2972) and grey in the blister pack (ref. 7590). The most amazing toy from this collection was the bathyscaph (ref. 7942). This pocket submarine could really dive and resurface thanks to a pull-switch connected by a tube. The Sea rescue set (ref. 2669) adapted from the 1967 *GI Joe* Breeches Buoy set, had in addition the orange lifejacket stamped with the emblem 'Sea Rescue' which in England, was *RNLI* (*RNLI* Sea Rescue set).

IN THE SNOW

It is 1978 that Joe and his team are really going to attack the frozen North with the Arctic Mission set, the sledge dogs and snowshoes. The skiing and the climbing had already been dealt with between 1976 and 1977, but not in such an intensive way. In 1979, a vehicle destined to travel on the ice floes[3] and a set for girls have closed this collection. Note that the canoe, meant for the Western, could be decorated in a contemporary manner with the suplied sheet of stickers.

IN THE AIR

The parachutist's outfits, which in fact include the helicopter and fighter pilot's helmets, dispose of parachutes that can really allow a figure to descend slowly from a window about two floors high. There were several helicopters. The yellow one from 76 changed to military green in 77 and was supplied with the sticker decorations for the Police and Fireman. In 1979, two other vehicles made their entry: First of all, the Condor FX –01 (ref. 2966), which is a vehicle composed of different modules. One can change the 3-wheeled undercarriage with two floats or better still, remove the wings and install two jet engines on the sides to have a very fast vehicle on land or water. The second vehicle, named the Capture Copter (ref. 4046) entered the French collection a bit like 'a hair in the soup' as it corresponds to an series non-commercialised in France (see Chapter *Before Action Joe*). It won't last long with *Action Joe* since it wasn't produced for more than a year.

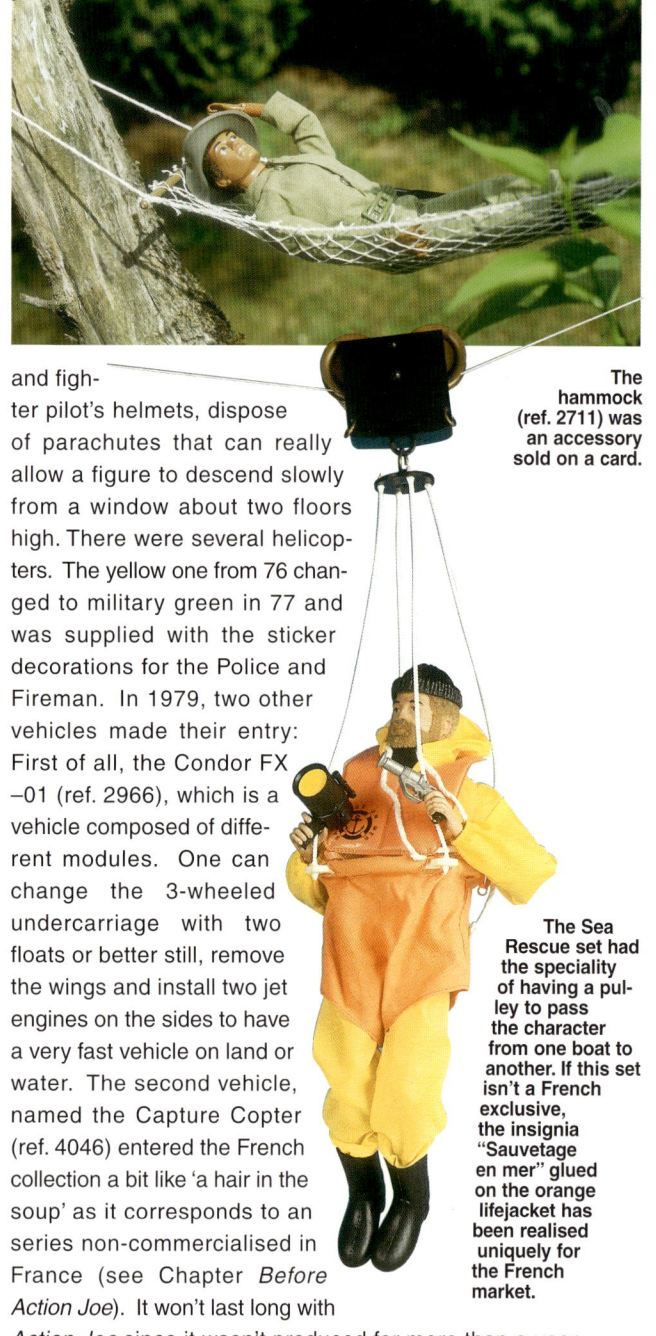

The hammock (ref. 2711) was an accessory sold on a card.

The Sea Rescue set had the speciality of having a pulley to pass the character from one boat to another. If this set isn't a French exclusive, the insignia "Sauvetage en mer" glued on the orange lifejacket has been realised uniquely for the French market.

---

[3]. The small tracked vehicle with its snow camouflage was in fact sold in England in the military range under the term 'Snowcat' and was produced with the Mountain Ranger equipment set. *Céji* stated that it was possible to repaint it for adventures in other latitudes.

The Cross-country on Motorbike set (ref. 4053) from 1979 was reproduced without the tool kit, to dress the figure Sam in 1980. The cross-country motorbike (ref. 4044) was produced at the same time as the set. It was available in five versions of different colours. Photo taken from the 1980 catalogue.

The Republican Guard (ref. 2974) was only commercialised for France and West Germany. There exists a colour variant of the jacket, which can be either dark blue or black.

The Second State Police motorbike (ref. 7987) and the first equipment set for the State Police motorcyclist (ref. 7911).

Fire Alert is the equipment set for the Paris fireman (ref. 7914) and his accessories: a fire-hose nozzle with water reservoir in a backpack (ref. 7943) dating from 1977.

43

The Speleologist (ref. 7908) was supplied with a lamp, which actually lit up.

In the Rockies (ref. 7917) was the version for girls with the outfit from Leader of the Rope Party. It was commercialised from 1977 onwards.

The canoe in its Adventure version (and not Western) with at its side, Joe in the 1978 Arctic Mission outfit (ref. 2667) and Daïna in the 1979 outfit from On the Icecap (ref. 2678).

To finish this enumeration of extraordinary vehicles, one mustn't forget the Delta wing, which appeared in 1977. It is a sort of delta glider to assemble, which can really glide in the air. Which make it, along with the bathyscaph, the perfect toys for outside games needing space and a stretch of water.

Left. **The all-purpose tracked vehicle (ref. 4033) in the frozen North version was only commercialised in 1979.**

The blister pack Polar Mission (ref. 2684) with snowshoes and small sledge.

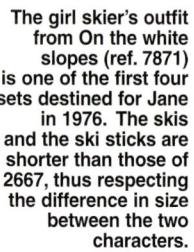

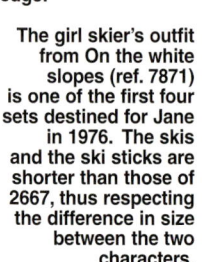

The girl skier's outfit from On the white slopes (ref. 7871) is one of the first four sets destined for Jane in 1976. The skis and the ski sticks are shorter than those of 2667, thus respecting the difference in size between the two characters.

44 *Below.* **The sledge and its two dogs from the Polar Expedition (ref. 2710).**

The secret agent 002 with his mask (ref. 7570) is an equipment set, which was only produced from 1976 to 1977. The suitcase contains a tape recorder, a long barrelled revolver and a grip for sharpshooters.

The karate kimono (ref. 7915) was only commercialised in 1977 then anew in 1979. This equipment set completes that of secret agent 002.

Opposite. The inflatable boat (ref. 7913) is stored in the rigid backpack, which has a compass on its flap cover. The paddle is removable and stores away in two bits at each side of the pack.

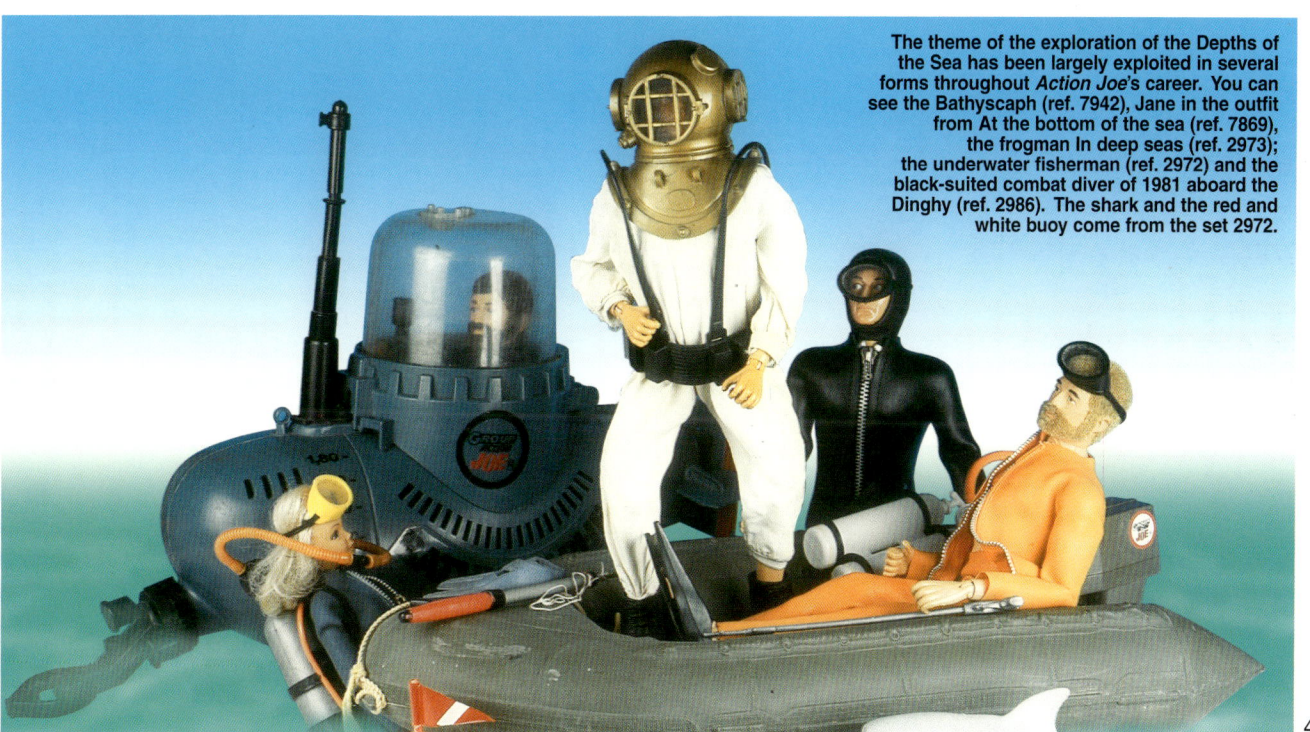

The theme of the exploration of the Depths of the Sea has been largely exploited in several forms throughout *Action Joe*'s career. You can see the Bathyscaph (ref. 7942), Jane in the outfit from At the bottom of the sea (ref. 7869), the frogman In deep seas (ref. 2973); the underwater fisherman (ref. 2972) and the black-suited combat diver of 1981 aboard the Dinghy (ref. 2986). The shark and the red and white buoy come from the set 2972.

45

WILD WEST

In 1976, little boys still liked to play at cowboys and Indians. It is why since the origin of the *Group Action Joe*, a cow-boy and an Indian were produced as action figures and were the subject of sets. A non-jointed, light-coloured horse was the sole accessory linked with these two heroes. *Céji* developed this theme very quickly, adding characters, outfits and accessories.

Once again, *Céji Arbois* showed the peaceful side of things with good relations between the Indians and cowboys. The revolvers were just part of the folklore and no conflict was evoked.

Since 1977, *Céji* used this environment to communicate widely. The cowboy was baptised Bill. The Indian was totally redesigned with the creation of new figures, Œil de Lynx accompanied by a Squaw, Daïna. The field widened with the creation of a tepee[1] (available between 1977 and 1979) then a canoe[2]. The second horse launched also in 1977 had Bill for illustration.

The Indians had much importance in French eyes as the accessories of Big Chief and of ceremony were commercialised in blister packs.

The evocation of the Far West is a European peculiarity since in the USA, *Hasbro* has not developed a cowboy or Indian set. The only *GI Joe* contribution to the Western range is the Canadian Mounted Police set. This uniform was first of all available for *GI Joe* in Canada in 1967. Then, one finds it in Great Britain distributed by *Palitoy* before making its appearance in France in 1977. France is also going to benefit from new references like Zorro and Davy Crockett. These two costumes bear the *Disney* copyright as they had been produced following a licence agreement between Céji and the film studio representatives. *Davy Crockett* and *Zorro* were two television series (with actors) produced by *Walt Disney*. *Zorro*'s outfit exists in numerous variants (silky or not silky clothes).

Céji distributed houses made of wood and hardboard from Germany to complete this collection. These houses produced under the *Schachfiguren für Reiseschach* label have never been presented in the *Action Joe* catalogues and have never carried the *Group* logo. This collection regrouped the Palace Saloon, the prison, the bank and the paddock. The paddock can accommodate two horses. The Palace Saloon is the biggest creation as it stands about one metre high and disposes of a second floor[3].

The high moment of the Western was between 1977 and 1979 for *Action Joe* as every year new references came to be added, with notably a special outfit for Jane in 1978.

In 1980, the Western is less successful, a whole generation of small children start to be interested, more and more, in space adventures. Sets like that of the US 7th Cavalry, of the Squaw or of Jane at Ranch J are going to disappear from the catalogue.

---

1. The tepee bears a lot of similarities to that of the *Lone Ranger Rides Again* toys developed around 1974 by *Marx* and distributed in Europe by *Gabriel*. The Indian tomahawks and the *Action Joe* holsters are also similar to those of the Lone Ranger action figures.

2. The canoe was delivered with a sheet of stickers to decorate it in three different ways: as an Indian canoe or a trapper's or an adventurer's (see previous chapter).

3. In fact, the first floor of the Palace Saloon is a bluff, as it doesn't allow one to stand the figures up in it, contrary to the ground floor, which is very spacious.

The cowboy has evolved during the existence of the *Group Action Joe*. In 1976, he still didn't have a name. It was possible to procure the set *(above)* or to buy the action figure *(left page)*. In 1977 he was baptised Bill, for all that the figure didn't change, nor his set which was named Bill in the Conquest of the West. From 1978 onwards, the figure will disappear. Alone the set endured and will evolve *(opposite right)* with a new hat, trousers more suited to horse riding and a whip. From 1976 to 1981, the *Group Action Joe* cowboys always wore the same red-checked shirt.

No cowboy without a mount! The rigid horse of 1976 (ref. 4541), which was taken from the '76 catalogue, will be replaced by an articulated Mustang from 1977 onwards (ref. 7960).

Centre right.
US 7th Cavalry equipment set 1978.

The Sheriff's set In the Name of the Law which was commercialised from 1977 onwards. The costume is richly detailed with a yellow shirt and a red fabric waistcoat. The hat is almost a sombrero (besides it will also serve for Zorro's set).

Jane has the right to a Far West set titled At Ranch J. Photo taken from the 1978 catalogue.

47

Canadian Mounted Police Set of 1977.

Zorro outfit of 1978.

Davy Crockett Set of 1977.

The canoe and its two versions for the Big West.

Above.
A variant exists for the Indian tunic.

Opposite.
The Indians have been the subjects of two sets, one for man in 76 and one for woman in 78 and of two accessories sets in 77.

48

The articulated eagle was always by the sides of the Indians.

The Tepee kit (ref. 7936) to assemble presented in the 1978 catalogue.

Two of the four Western houses distributed in France by Céji Arbois around 1977. The Palace Saloon (ref. 4114) *(above)* and the horse shelter (ref. 4118) *(left)*.

These 1/6 models were to assemble. The different panels of wood and hardwood are held together by red wooden pins. These models were not included in the *Group Action Joe* range but they were certainly conceived for action figures.

49

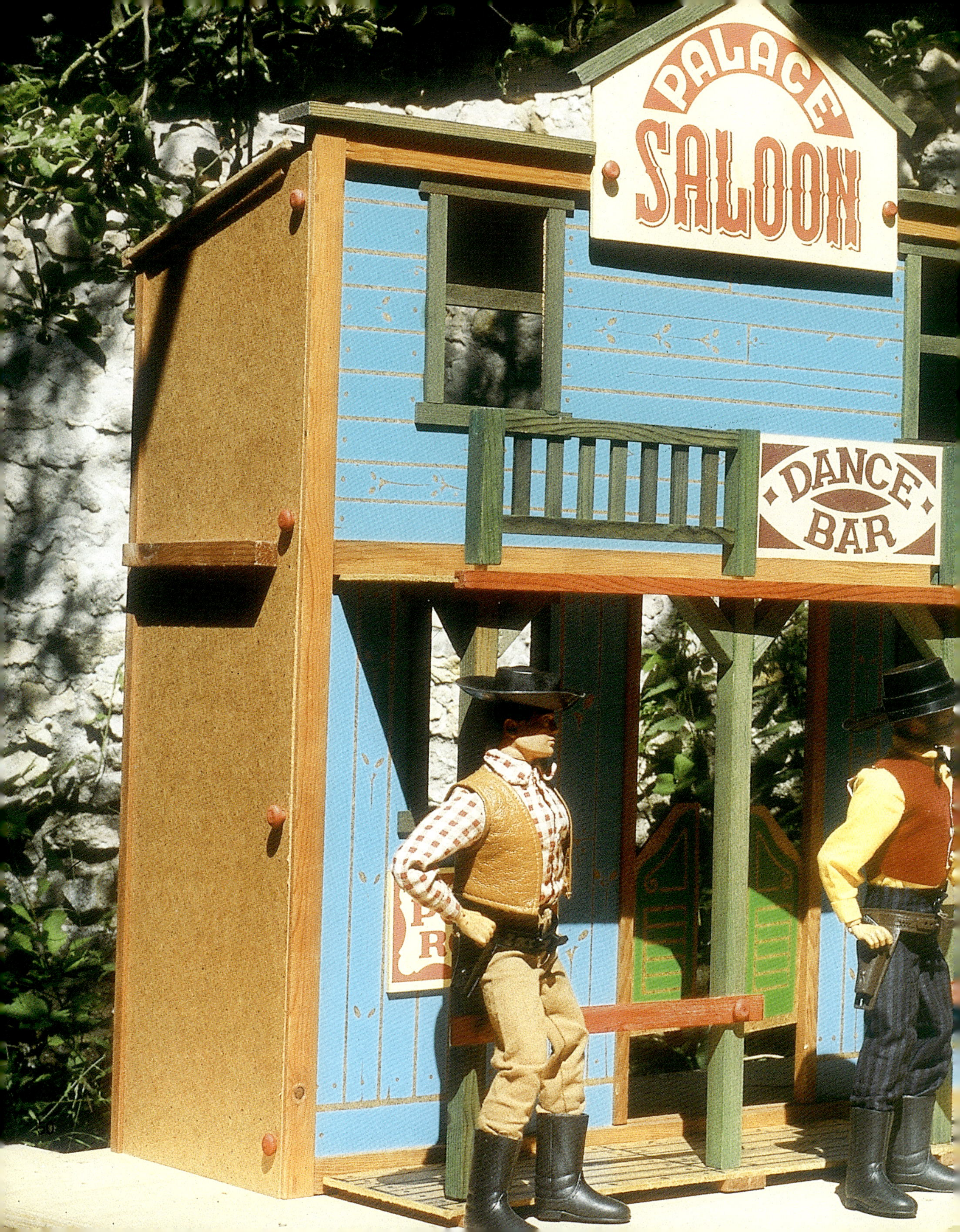
PALACE
SALOON
DANCE
BAR

51

OUTER SPACE

Space Conquest, the astronaut's equipment set commercialised in France only between 1979 and the end of 1980 (ref. 4031).

Science fiction and the spatial adventure are the basis for the fourth field, which only appeared in the *Group Action Joe* in 1980.

The arrival on the small screen of *Goldorak* (*UFO robot Grendizer*), followed by *Albator* (*French name for Captain Harlock*), *Capitaine Flam* (*French name for Captain Future*) and *Battles of the Planets* has developed children's tastes.

The mode changes, the science fiction begins to prevail over the Adventure and the Far West. This tendency is felt very quickly in toy manufacturing. *Céji Arbois*, who is familiar with toys under licences of cartoon films, is going to distribute toys coming from these new television series.

Already in 1979, the set Space Conquest had made its arrival in the catalogue under the reference 4031. It involved the reuse of the American spacesuit from the Mercury Missions, which were commercialised in the USA and Great Britain from 1967 onwards. In 1979, *Céji* also produced an action figure, Albator, using the *Action Joe* body.

«*Cosmos 2080, Action Joe and his Group are going to experience fantastic adventures and to discover new worlds. Radian, their interstellar ship will take them to unknown planets where they will be able to go on reconnaissance in their super, all-purpose, planetary exploration vehicle, Stratos, and to travel through these worlds, full of promise and great expectations…*» The spatial collection was presented like that in the 1980 catalogue.

It is impossible to speak of this collection without mentioning *Super Joe* and the toys, *Alcor* and *Actarus*, heroes from *Goldorak*. For all the accessories of the *Goldorak* range came from the American *Super Joe*. We will find some of these devices repainted in the silver version of the *Group Action Joe* space range.

SUPER JOE

A look back! The 12-inch *GI Joe* was abandoned in the USA at the end of 1976 to the benefit of a new orientation of Hasbro towards smaller action figures. *Super Joe*[1], who had a body of about 9 inches (or 25 cm) was close to the 1/8 scale and had a particularly short career. *Super Joe* had adopted the same size as that of *Big Jim* from *Mattel*. Also he disposed of a mechanism in his back permitting him to move his arms so as to give a karate chop.

In France, *Action Joe* preserved his height of 12-inches corresponding to the 1/6 scale. In any case, the French boys and girls could between 1978 and 1979, play with *Super Joe* without knowing it. *Céji Arbois* having obtained the *Goldorak* licence reproduced the two humans, Actarus and Alcor from *Super Joe*'s body. Moreover, one can see the logo composed of an interlaced S and a T engraved on their belt buckle and hidden under the baize of their red or blue uniform. Later, *Céji Arbois* used simplified versions of Super Joe to create a Captain Future and a Mark from the *Battles of the Planets*. The chests of these last figures were no longer jointed and they didn't have mechanisms to move the arms. *Super Joe*'s spatial, all-purpose machine was also used in France by *Céji Arbois* to become the ship for *Alcor* and *Actarus*.

---

[1]. The bodies of *Super Joe* suffer the same problems with ageing of the rubber joints and flexible hands. Professor Kelp has published advice on repairs in the magazines *Dixième Planète* N° 29 and 30 (June and August 2004).

The action figures Alcor and Actarus used the figures and accessories of the *Super Joe* American range. The accessories will be reused for the *Group Action Joe* in 1980.

American *Super Joe* sets.

The Rocket Command Centre, which in France will become the Cosmic Station for *Alcor* and *Actarus*.

53

The power generator (ref. 7965 sold on card) was the adaptation of the model from the *Super Joe* range used by Alcor and Actarus.

The space diver from Captain Harlock crew (in the cartoon) inspired the Space Pirate equipment set (ref. 7948). The skull and crossbones emblem was the same as that of the figure in Space Privateer.

The *Super Joes* disposed of an original accessory: a power generator. It involved a harness with an electric bulb placed on the torso and a battery compartment for one AA battery in the back. This accessory had a plug to connect it to other tools in order to supply power for their motor. This generator (black for the *Goldorak* toys) was modified for the *Action Joes*.

It has been enlarged to correspond with the measurements of the 12-inch figures and painted in metallic grey, which is a peculiarity of the French market. *Céji Arbois* had used certain *Palitoy* elements, like the Space Ranger or the spaceship but this was not the case for the power harness developed by *Palitoy* for *Action Man*.

The Turbocopter (ref. 7967) that locks onto the harness.

The laser gun accessory (ref. 7981) contains a lamp, which lights up when connected to the generator.

54

The 'ultrasound radar' (ref. 7968) with instructions.

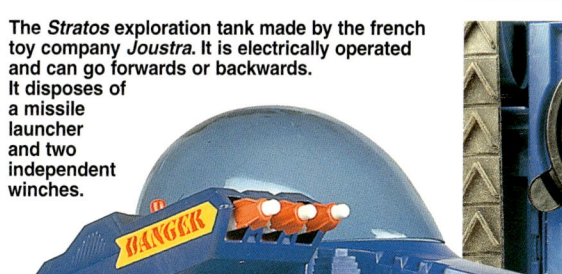

The *Stratos* exploration tank made by the french toy company *Joustra*. It is electrically operated and can go forwards or backwards. It disposes of a missile launcher and two independent winches.

55

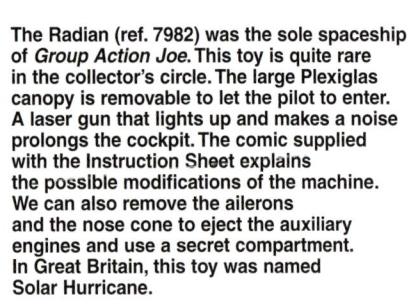

The Radian (ref. 7982) was the sole spaceship of *Group Action Joe*. This toy is quite rare in the collector's circle. The large Plexiglas canopy is removable to let the pilot to enter. A laser gun that lights up and makes a noise prolongs the cockpit. The comic supplied with the Instruction Sheet explains the possible modifications of the machine. We can also remove the ailerons and the nose cone to eject the auxiliary engines and use a secret compartment. In Great Britain, this toy was named Solar Hurricane.

Captain Cosmos

The *Group Action Joe*'s universe 'Space' rests principally on Mark alias Captain Cosmos. There, *Céji* has a 'home-made' hero who is accompanied by a spaceship, an exploration machine and several accessories. The set, Space Conquest is integrated in this collection. The Space Pirate set permits the creation of adventures with a 'baddie' all found.

The accessories are three in number and all function with the power generator. We find the turbocopter and the ultrasound radar (sold in a box) and a laser gun (sold on a card), which are not taken from *Super Joe*.

The Space Pirate set arises from a sort of 'do-it yourself' assembly, since it reuses the astronaut's helmet, painted black and his hand weapon is Albator's pistol. The pirate's emblem on his overalls is that of Albator. His 'laser gun' is in fact an element coming from the flame-thrower, which accompanies the tropical outfit for the soldier.

Stratos

The all-purpose, planetary exploration tank of *Group Action Joe* was a motorised toy. Just like the 4x4 Fighter, the Stratos was originally a *Joustra*[2] toy. Its tracks were operated by a battery-powered motor, which could be disengaged in order to avoid breaking the wheel mechanisms. A plastic cabin capped with a translucent bubble tops this model, which is in metal. This cabin could hold a driver. It is armed with a directional missile launcher. It is equipped with two front winches. The missiles are of an equivalent model to those used by the *Shogun Warrior Goldorak*, which was distributed by *Mattel*. The 1980 catalogue announced two Stratos models, a motorised version (ref. 7975) and a single-band remote controlled version (ref. 7974). This last, which differed by its aerial, was not commercialised.

Radian

The interstellar vessel of *Group Action Joe* was named the Radian. It resembles a single-manned fighter and sports the colours of Captain Cosmos, the Space Ranger. It is his personal ship. It disposes of a quite restricted 'son et lumière' function. Its two auxiliary engines can be ejected. A secret hiding place behind the pilot's seat permits one to store the accessories for Captain Cosmos.

Of British conception, this machine at the same epoch was available under the name Solar Hurricane in the *Action Man* range from *Palitoy* with different sticker decorations (Space Ranger). At the back of the Instructions Sheet, there was a space adventure comic in black and white, with Captain Cosmos. The Space range of *Group Action Joe* will not experience any changes in 1981, apart from the disappearance of the astronaut's set. The Stratos tank will continue to be available after the end of *Group Action Joe* in the *Action Man* collection, which will follow in 1982.

---

2. The Stratos had been given the place of honour by way of a competition game (see chapter Stars & Competitions).

U.S. Patent   Feb. 1, 1977   4,00

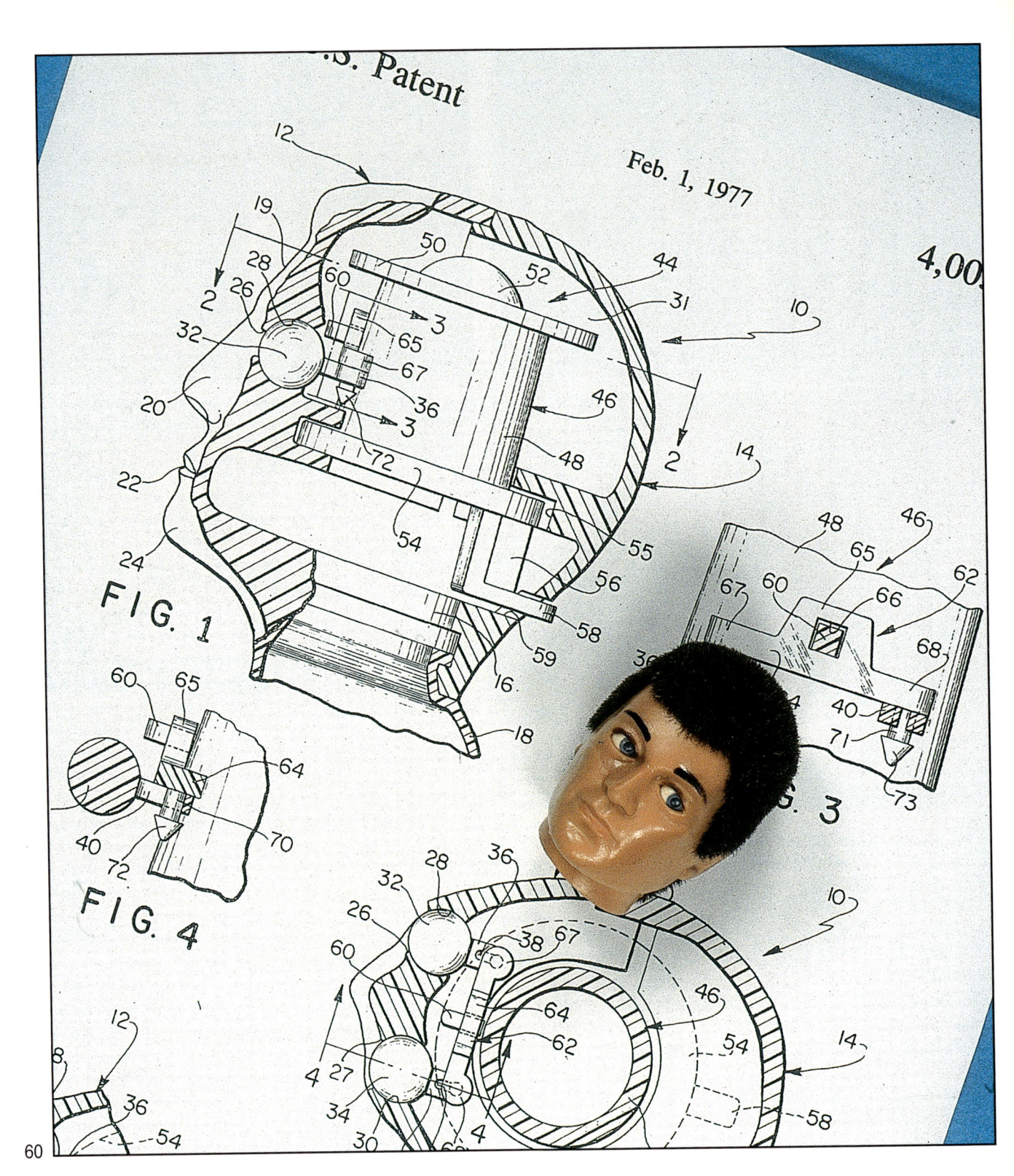

Opposite.
The mechanism for the movable eyes (Eagle Eyes) has a specific Patent.

Right.
Variation concerning the engraving on the girls' shorts.

same sculpture and practically the same proportions as their former models with flock hair. They are rigid as they contain a whole tangle of small parts linking the pull knob at the back of the skull to the eyes whilst totally avoiding the neck-joint pin.

SOME SUPER GIRLS!

Curiously, very little information exists about the female bodies. All that one knows is that Jane, Peggy and Daïna all have the same body. This model was launched on the French market at the end of 1976. Despite the information 'Patent Pending' engraved on the figures' backs, indicating that a patent had been applied for, I have not found any trace of a Patent concerning them.

Without doubt because the female body has the same characteristics as the 1975 Muscle Body and it is strictly impossible to patent the same invention twice.

The head is supple and it engages with the stump of the neck, a current way of fixing the head onto the body of the Barbie-type dolls. The attachment of the rigid head to Jane with movable eyes is formed from the 1975 model of the male body.

It is the same for the rest of the joints composed of rubber parts for all the girls. The shorts are black and have the A and the T, from *Adventure Team*, interlaced on the left side.

In 1976 Jane's shorts are smooth whereas the models that follow from 1977 onwards comprise of a sort of engraved thread.

ACTION MAN

In 1979, a newcomer joins the team of Joe and his comrades in adventure. It concerns a blond pilot with movable eyes. He will be baptised Sam. If his face was that of Bob with blond hair, his body was absolutely new.

Slimmer than the others, he had the peculiarity of having a sole rubber part to hold together the neck and the chest. All the others are entirely in plastic. More robust (these bodies are still in perfect state, except for the neck, at the present time) this model is of *Palitoy* origin.

For proof, the belt buckle of his plastic shorts sports the British logo of *Action Man*. It will be the same for other characters that follow, like Mark Captain Cosmos.

This new body made its appearance in England at the same time as in France. Its conception goes back to 1977 and *CPG Products Corp* patented it. It will be the official successor to *Action Joe* in 1982, when *Miro Meccano* continues the line by distributing some of the *Palitoy Action Man* range.

The girls' hands were simpler. Jane's head with movable eyes disposed of the same mechanism as that of the men's head.

The 1979 *Action Man*'s body (below) with the British logo on the belt buckle.

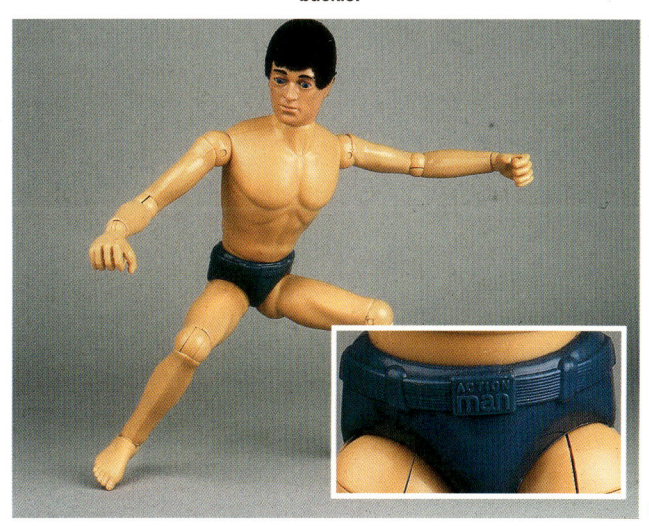

61

STARS & COMPETITIONS

In order to attract young customer loyalty and encourage consumer spending, *Céji Arbois* had recourse to two methods, one consisted of gaining brand loyalty by offering stars to collect as proof of purchase and the other in regularly organising game competitions. In both cases, it was possible to win *Action Joe* products.

THE STARS

The number of stars printed on the packaging varied according to the toy's value. For example, an action figure provided one or two stars, one only for a set in blister pack and two stars if in a box. As for the vehicles, it was the jackpot with sometimes five stars on one box. The children had to cut them out and stick them on the collector's booklet available in the shop. Once filled, one simply had to post it to *Céji Arbois* to be sure of receiving a gift.

The number of stars varied between 23 and 27 according to the period and on the forms, there were always two or three stars already printed, so that one didn't start from zero and to give hope of completing the collection. Those who did so were not disappointed because in most cases, they received a set or a figure.

THE COMPETITIONS

Between 1980 and 1981, *Céji* developed two competitions by way of children's magazines and toyshops at the same time.

In 1980, *Céji Arbois* released the big game 'The Bermuda Triangle', a competition in conjunction with children's publications and toy shops (*The Journal de Mickey*, 15th and 19th April, *Pif Gadget*, 15th and 22nd April and the 6th May).

This game, which ended on the 17th May 1980, consisted of reconstructing a secret message related to the ultra-confidential plans for the completely new space exploration vehicle, the Stratos.

The participants must stick together the two halves of a message. The first half, found in the pages of the two editions of Mickey and the three editions of Pif, had to be cut out and matched up with the second half printed on a reply coupon available in the toy shops. One could also read «*The secret of the Stratos planet explorer is…*» in the magazines.

In fact, it was the second half of the message, which was most important. There existed four combinations, which according to their rarity allowed the children to obtain a prize more or less important, from a sticker to a pocket submarine.

Combination A «*His Missile Launcher*» was worth a Bermuda Triangle sticker, Combination B «*the existence of 2 winches at the front of the vehicle*» was rewarded by a Bermuda Triangle poster, the holder of Combination C «*his flight deck with movable cockpit*» obtained a figure and finally, the rare Combination D «*his electric version*» permitted one to win a pocket submarine, that's to say, the deep water diving module (bathyscaph).

The toyshop awarded the prize straightaway. That was but the 'first chance'. The second chance lay in the participation of a lottery, by way of the bulletin found in the brochure. The prizes of this second chance were allotted in the following manner:

1st prize: A Stratos prototype accompanied by a toy box filled with action figures, accessories and vehicles of the same brand.

2nd to 51st prizes: A special box containing the crew who participated in the secret mission *The Bermuda Triangle*, that's to say, the diver and skin-divers (men and women).

52nd to 1051st prizes: An action figure.

The aim of this competition was to push the children to go into the shops to search for the other half of the message, the secret messages, which boasted the qualities of the new product that was the completely new Stratos tank.

The last competition was *Operation Niagara* in 1981. There again, *Céji Arbois* pulled out all the stops to make a big hit. A blister pack of accessories was offered to every participant who drew his entrance form for the lottery. This original blister pack was entitled 'Free blister pack with First Aid Kit' surmounted by the title, *Operation Niagara* and contained a distress rocket launcher, a pair of binoculars and a nurse's white bag stamped with the red cross.

The pretext of this game was an adventure in the middle of a natural catastrophe. An earthquake near the Niagara Falls provoked heavy flooding and the *Group Action Joe* intervenes to bring aid to the population. Swimmers, speleologists, military, adventurers, helicopter, tent and dinghy are mobilised (that's to say the biggest part of the toy collection).

The first prize of the draw was the complete *Action Joe* Collection and the next 1000 winners were offered an action figure. This game ended on 22nd April 1981, just a few months before the *Group Action Joe* disappeared to give way to *Action Man*.

First star collection booklet.

Stars to cut out.

The competition which appeared in *Pif Gadget* and the *Journal de Mickey* between April and May 1980 always contained the same first part of the message *(opposite left)*. Only the second part printed in the brochures available in toyshops varied *(below)*. Here is the most common answer, which allowed one to win a sticker.

First Aid worker's booklet to complete with stars in order to receive a free action figure, without outfits, during 1981. The booklet is full.

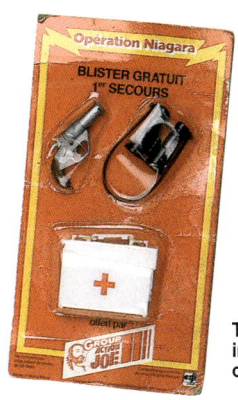

Sticker offered to participants in the *Bermuda Triangle* game.

The 'First Aid' set on card offered free in toyshops during the period of the Operation Niagara game.

ADVERTISING

The *Group Action Joe* benefited from tremendous publicity campaigns using a lot of creativity to advance the originality and richness of the toys in the collection. These numerous advertisements have become the real childhood memory joggers for a good number of nostalgic collectors.

The French firm principally targeted two children's periodicals, *Pif Gadget* and the *Journal de Mickey*. *Pif Gadget* is a comic magazine sold with a toy to construct. *Pif Gadget* has known great popularity in France and has been re-edited since the summer of 2004. One also found commercials in other magazines like *Tintin* and *Télé Junior*.

ADVERTISING CAMPAIGNS

It was through the written press that *Céji Arbois* could best inform the children of the launch of his annual collections. The idea was to present *Action Joe* as an original toy and not as an extension of *Action Man*. The arrival of new comrades in adventure was announced by the publicitys, which gave the preview of the new toy and its characteristics. So firstly, *Action Joe* was defined as an invincible hero (who was still brown and beardless). Joe explained that he measured 29 cm (12"), he was fully articulated, his hands could grip, he disposed of numerous outfits, of hundreds of accessories and a complete group of comrades. This first publicity was accompanied by a bulletin to cut out and take to a toy shop to receive a free sticker. Once the introductions were done, the *Action Joe* publicity could begin to show Joe and his comrades in action with photos re-uniting accessories, outfits, vehicles and intermingled characters, one could not yet distinguish the different references, but the public could quickly understand the multiple games possibilities offered by this new toy.

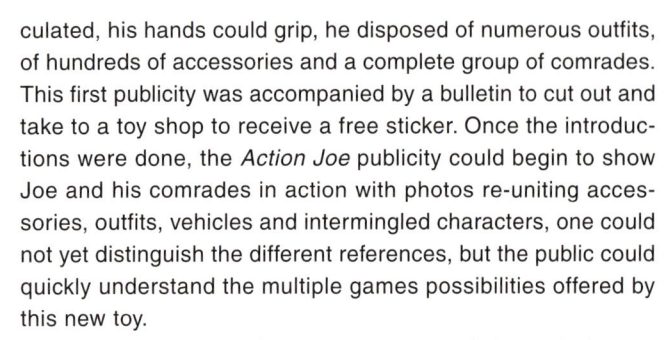

It is in 1977 that the *Group Action Joe* really 'explodes' at the publicity level. The make is known to the retailers, the public start to become attached to the new idea, *Céji* has just redesigned the packaging and logo to achieve a hundred percent French identity and decides to launch a big campaign for the first half of 77 with three 'announces-posters' (to use the *Céji* managers' catch phrase at that time). These advertisements were designs accompanied by some photos of boxes and close-ups boasting the movable eyes, the life like hair and beard implants and the stick-on tattoos supplied with Œil de Lynx, occupied two full pages of the principal children's magazines. The first advertisement, which staged the complete *Group* in a Karate Hall, was published first of all on the 29th March 1977 in *Tintin*, then on the 2nd April in the *Journal de Mickey* and finally the 6th April in *Pif Gadget*. It is without doubt the greatest publicity for the *Group Action Joe*. In order to remember well, the nine comrades' names, a sheet of stickers with portrait medallions of each was offered by toy retailers. The second advertisement concerned the Wild West. It was launched in April, in the same three publications. The third chosen field was that of the Paris firemen, with a poster of a fire with close ups of the brand new fireman's set and the possibility of painting the Land Rover and helicopter red. This campaign ended with

Here how Joe made his appearance in the children's press in 1976. He was nicknamed the 'Invincible' and the range isn't yet detailed.

ACTION JOE, L'INVINCIBLE... Mieux qu'un jouet, un monde d'aventures...

the last publication of the fire poster on the 4th May in the *Journal de Mickey*. It was resumed by the dispatch of posters to the shops, which also relayed the effect of the advertisements to obtain an efficient synergy. The publicity designs continued during the second semester with half page adverts starring the Delta wing and the Radio Communications Centre.

After that the advertisements change their style. Diorama photos replaced the designs. It is the firm *Créateurs Associés*, which is charged with production of the perilous situations that are commented on by the celebrated phrase «…*What is Action Joe going to do?*».

These impressive productions necessitated, just like the catalogues, numerous hours of work in the photo studio. They gave all the originality to the *Group Action Joe*, which distinguished itself from other toys of that same period. Rahan had the right to a page all to himself, published – as of course-in *Pif Gadget*.

In later times (between 1980 and 1981)

Here a general idea of the commercials from the end of 1976 and the beginning of 1977. The photos of the first figures show numerous possibilities of games and mission themes to accomplish.
Two other commercials are the Fire and the Western themes published in *Tintin*, *Journal de Mickey* and *Pif Gadget* between April and May 1977.
The third publicity of this campaign can be seen on the next two pages.

Joe et Œil de Lynx ont les yeux qui bougent !

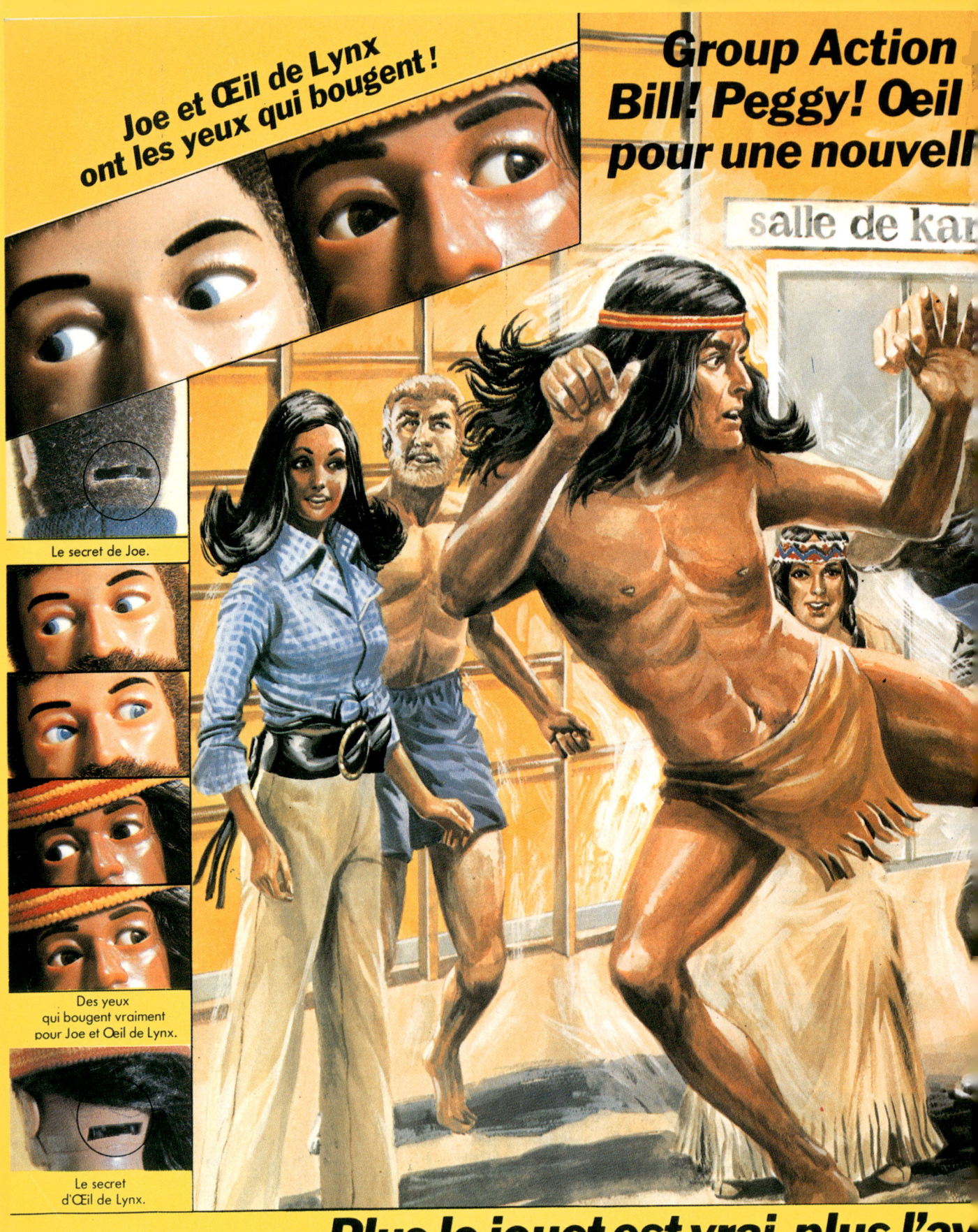

Group Action
Bill! Peggy! Oeil
pour une nouvell[e]

salle de kar[até]

Le secret de Joe.

Des yeux qui bougent vraiment pour Joe et Œil de Lynx.

Le secret d'Œil de Lynx.

Plus le jouet est vrai, plus l'av[enture]

• Tom! Sam! Jane! Daïna! Bob!
ynx! • Joe entraîne ses hommes
ission. Laquelle?
A toi de décider.

9 compagnons.

JOE • ŒIL DE LYNX
TOM • BILL
SAM • BOB
JANE • PEGGY
DAÏNA

Des dizaines de panoplies,
d'accessoires
et de véhicules.
Va vite les voir chez ton
marchand de jouets.

GROUP ACTION JOE

Jouets CEJI arbois

ure est vraie.

The complex productions «What is Action Joe going to do?» date from 1979 and were also published in the *Télé Junior* magazine. Others coveted them besides children.
The designs for the Radio Communication centre appeared in *Pif Gadget* in November 1977.
The series of commercials 'Invent the Adventure' put Rahan in the foreground twice.
The publicity, produced in the shape of photos, which tell a story, relates Tom's underwater rescue of Daïna dating from the end of 1980.

'Ambush in the Amazon',
'The Bermuda Trap', 'Ambuscade on Alpa'
and 'Onwards for new adventures'
are the last commercials published
in 1981.

the advertising amounted to half-page adverts presenting the characters in much less dynamic situations.

On television

Around 1978, the publicity spots combining real actors playing the part of the members of *Group Action Joe* with the toys were diffused during the advertising slots in emissions for young spectators. At the time, the regulations dictated that only toys made in Europe could be presented in television commercials. That is why *Céji* only presented some *Action Joe* toys like the all-purpose vehicle (the six-wheeled vehicle was made in Spain by *Geyper*), the four-wheel drive Fighter (made in France by *Joustra*) or the helicopter (made in the UK by *Palitoy*). These commercials showed actors who resembled and dressed like the action figures. They showed the way before being replaced by the actual action figures. This technique is found in the *Action Man* commercials between 1995 and 2002.

69

AFTER ACTION JOE 1982-2004

**In 1982, Action Man supplanted Action Joe for a short period, which will end in 1984.
The figurines of nearly 4-inches (10 cm) were justified action figures. GI Joe continued his career in France with this scale for several years. Then just like the Phoenix, GI Joe and Action Man reappeared at the dawn of the thirtieth anniversary of the birth of the 'Movable Fighting Man' to experience a second youth.**

The *Hasbro* licence, which permitted *Céji Arbois* to manufacture and distribute *Action Joe*, had ended on the 1st January 1982. The French firm *Miro Meccano* had recuperated the *Hasbro* toys. For several years already *Meccano* distributed the *Kenner* toys with the *Star Wars* collection of figurines. As from the beginning of 1982, *Miro Meccano* announced to the professionals the arrival of *Action Man* presented as an improved version of *Action Joe*. It concerned in fact some of the toys that *Palitoy* distributed in England at the same epoch. The figures were essentially the men with movable eyes sold in 'closed' boxes. So one rediscovers the adventurer, the diver, the Space Ranger or simply a figure without clothes. Only Zargon was a true newcomer. Zargon is an extra-terrestrial pirate whose arm is none other than the sabre of Albator. Some sets survived the change of distributor (Red Beret Para, Mountain Ranger, US Machine Gunner, Frogman, State Police). Others were new like that of the modern English Fantassin, Space Ranger or the totally modified Space Pirate. Three futuristic sets regrouped under the term Special Force were produced in luxurious coffrets. Arms and accessories (of which the special operation's pack and rack) were still available. Later, overalls and jackets were available in blister packs.

The military helicopter was armed with four missiles and a machi-

The letter from *Céji Arbois* to his clients, explaining that *Action Joe* is no longer distributed by his company

Two *Action Man* in version 'without clothes' sold from 1982 onwards. The hair colour (brown or blond) was not stated on the box.

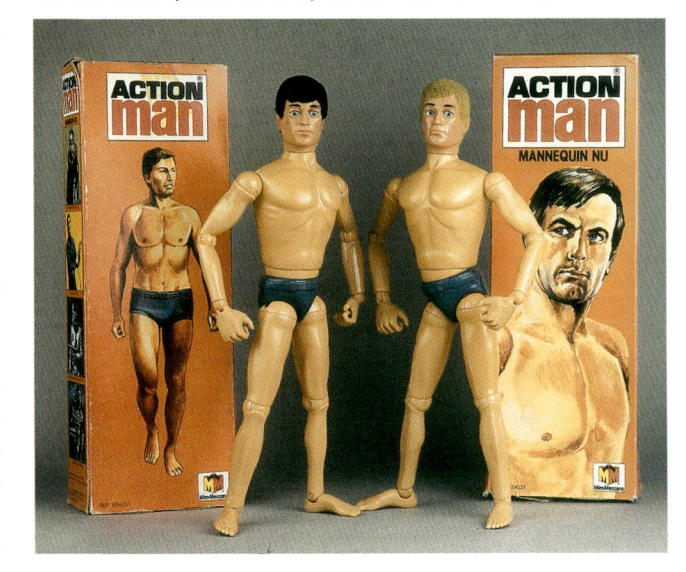

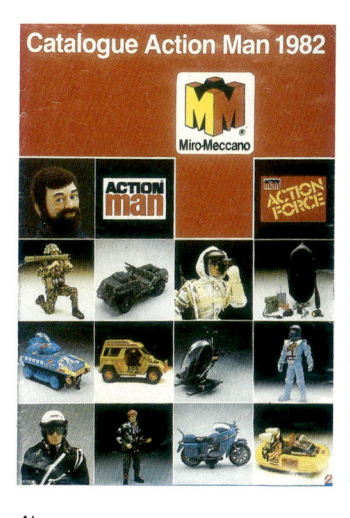

Above.
The 1982 *Action Man* catalogue destined for the toy professionals. In it, *Miro Meccano* indicates that «*Action Joe gives birth to Action Man*». *Action Force* was presented for the first time. A competition with prizes of video tape recorders and Stratos tanks was organised for the launch of *Action Man*.

Far right.
Zargon, the enemy of Action Man in 1982.

Below and right.
The Special Team was composed of three futuristic sets: Polar Commando, Diver Commando and Fantassin Commando (presented in the 1982 professionals' catalogue).

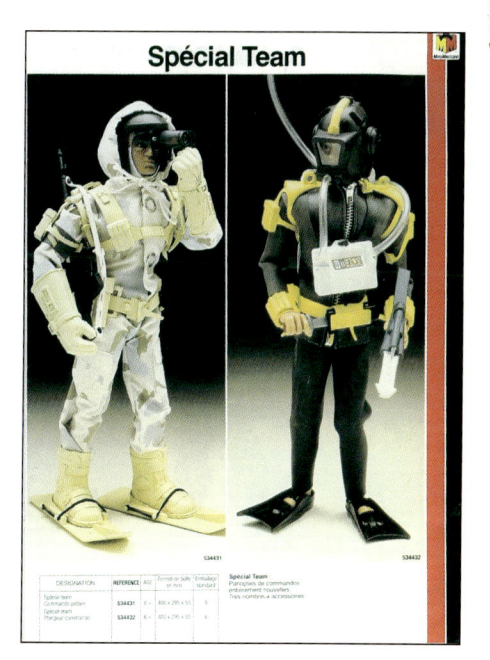

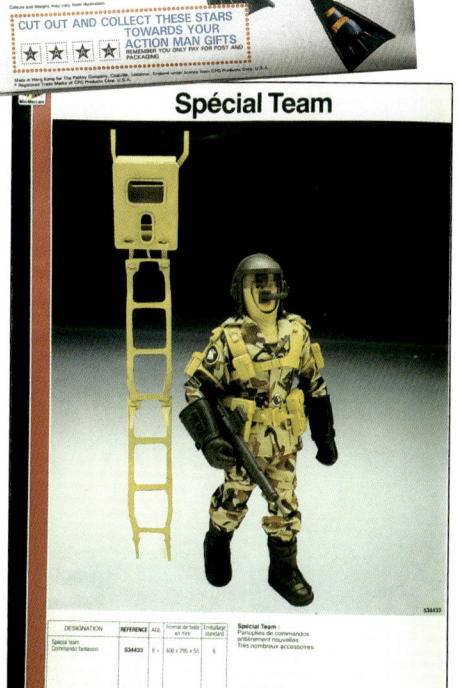

71

Action Man clothes on cards, which were available in France towards 1983.

Action Man SAS: Latest innovation from Palitoy available in France by Miro Meccano. It was in British packaging with the addition of a sticker in black and white destined to translate the inscriptions, contents of the box, indicate the distributor's name and address and to notify the reference in the French catalogue. The SAS Commander who could talk was not distributed in France (without doubt because of the language problem).

ne gun from now on. A Jeep had replaced the Landrover. We will find the Police motorbike and the Stratos originating from *Group Action Joe*. The toys were distributed then in new packaging decorated with the 1966 emblem. The 1982 *Action Man* references were much less numerous. To mark the grand arrival of *Action Man*, *Miro Meccano* launched a competition putting in front a brown figure with movable eyes dressed in a plain white T-shirt decorated with the *Action Man* logo. A way of making us forget the good old *Action Joe*? Not sure, because at the back of this document we still find the logo '*Group Action Joe*'.

Action Man ended his career in France when *Palitoy* stopped production in Great Britain. In latter times, a new theme had been developed with the SAS[1]. The figures in military strike outfits, the black dinghy, the helicopter (in black commando version with floats) and sets were available in France in English packaging. *Meccano* contenting itself by simply adding a sticker carrying its name and address.

THE MINIATURISATION

The *GI Joe* of about ten centimetres didn't arrive immediately in France[2]. First of all there was *Action Force*. Of English conception, *Action Force* progressively replaced *Action Man* at *Palitoy* from 1982 onwards. It was the same thing in France. The first year concerned characters wearing uniforms that corresponded to the sets of figures. Then the *Action Force* label became totally independent with themes

---

1. The SAS, Special Air Service is an elite British Intervention Corps formed by highly trained commandos, which was created in 1942 during the World War II. Their motto is «*Who dares wins*».

2. The *GI Joe* 3 3/4", in the scale 1/18, toys have for their label «*GI Joe, the Real American Hero*».

The first 3 3/4" action figures, which were commercialised in France in 1982, were not those of *GI Joe*, but those of *Action Force*.

The return of the 12-inch *GI Joe* in the USA was marked by these four figures that came from the cartoon film, in Europe they were sold under the *Action Man* Label.

1994 *Action Man* with 'real' hair.

Opposite. Natalie and Knuck, the two friends of *Action Man* are European exclusives.

Some references commercialised in France in these recent years.

The James Bond coffrets render homage to the films, *Thunderball, Tomorrow Never Dies, Goldeneye,* and *The Spy Who Loved Me. Action Man* wears in turn, a diver's outfit, a dinner jacket, a Russian nuclear scientist's overalls, Commando fatigues and a skiing outfit.

approaching Science Fiction. The vehicles became more and more delirious and came closer to those developed by *Hasbro* in the USA. At last in 1986, the 'small' *GI Joes* arrived in France with the success of the cartoon film. This toy touched a new generation of children who were ignorant of all the earlier *GI Joes* and who had not played with *Action Joes*.

Renaissance

In September 1991 in the USA, the Target shop chain tried 'a hit' in proposing in a limited series, a 12-inch action figure of Duke, the hero of the *GI Joe* cartoon. This creation uses a new, more muscular body and accessories much less detailed than those of the 60's and 70's. The gun disposes of an electronic sound. This action figure knows a quick success (sold out in two weeks). *Hasbro* decides to launch a limited collection, *Hall of Fame* with four characters (Duke, Cobra Commander, Snake Eyes and Stalker) in June 1992. These four characters were commercialised in different packaging in France in 1993. Although the *GI Joes* had become popular with the cartoon, the name Action Man came out of the cupboard because, in European minds, the 12-inch are the *Action Man* and the 3 3/4" are the *GI Joe*. Moreover, this idea is so strong that the press file of that epoch leaves us to understand that «*Action Man is the ancestor of GI Joe*». We know the rest. *GI Joe* leaves the place to *Action Man* who disposes of a specific range and a modernised black and orange logo. But that isn't only for Europe. In the USA, the 12-inch figures also make a comeback, but under the form of figures in commemorative collections. Sometimes

The re-editions of the 1964 *GI Joe* products especially for the collector's market in the USA.

The talking *Action Man*.

it concerns re-editions of models from the sixties. The Hall of Fame range is going to develop, which won't prevent the small figures to continue their life. Since then the 12-inch continue to be developed with sometimes, original creations like Buzz Aldrin, the General George Washington or J-F. Kennedy. Several collections are run at the same time. Lastly, the first four *GI Joes* (soldier, Marine, pilot and sailor) were produced with their original sets in '40th Anniversary' coffrets for collectors.

Action Man, the greatest of all heroes

The new 1994 *Action Man* is in step with the times. He is meant for children of around 4 to 7 years. His look, his logo and packaging are totally redesigned. Orange becomes the predominant colour. At first, he has been a sort of secret agent teaming up with a woman (Natalie) and a tough (Knuck) who are both unique action figures. An enemy is invented to 'play opposite' to the heroes, he is Doctor X (the heir of Captain Zargon of the eighties from *Palitoy*?). A cartoon series was produced to re-launch the mode and touch a new generation of consumers. A real actor performed the introduction and the ending of the cartoon. The fact of having the role of an action figure played by an actor is not new, remember the television commercials for *Action Joe*, a style taken up again for the recent *Action Man* adver-

3. For the surprises and free gifts, *Action Man* has been produced under the form of miniature figurines.

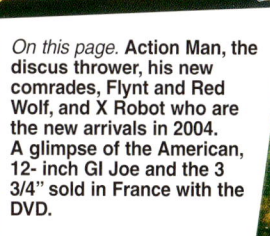

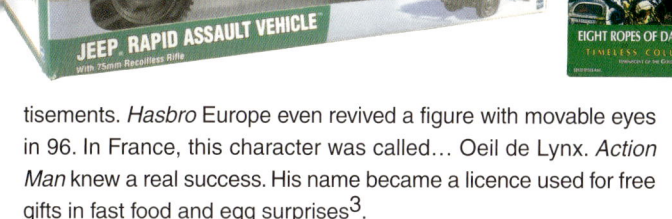

On this page. **Action Man**, the discus thrower, his new comrades, Flynt and Red Wolf, and X Robot who are the new arrivals in 2004. A glimpse of the American, 12- inch GI Joe and the 3 3/4" sold in France with the DVD.

tisements. *Hasbro* Europe even revived a figure with movable eyes in 96. In France, this character was called… Oeil de Lynx. *Action Man* knew a real success. His name became a licence used for free gifts in fast food and egg surprises[3].

With the years, *Action Man* moves more towards the extreme sports. A new cartoon series is in the making. This time it concerns a digital cartoon in 3D.

The modern bodies of *GI Joe* and *Action Man* will equally serve for other action figures that *Hasbro* is going to produce under licence. The best known figures are very clearly the *Star Wars* heroes. *Action Man* embodied the most celebrated British secret agent in 1998. Presented in numbered coffrets, an *Action Man* wore the different *James Bond* outfits according to his films.

The big difference between the modern *Action Man* and his original 'big brother' is that now it is no longer possible to change the figure's outfits. A diver will always be a diver, a racing driver will always be a racing driver. In future, one buys a figure for his son like one bought a set in the past.

THE 12-INCH MODE

For his part the original *GI Joe* has become a museum piece, which is the subject of conventions, veritable messes in the honour of the brave soldiers who made several generations of children dream.

An American firm, *Cotswold*, has even specialised in the line production of replicas of accessories, spare parts and the bodies of *GI Joe* from the sixties under the *Elite Brigade* label, in order to permit collectors to restore or complete their troops. The size of this action figure has been adopted by hundreds of manufacturers during the past forty years and the 12-inch figures have become at the same time, subjects of collection and a source of inspiration for artists.

IN OUR DAYS

Since the beginning of 2003, *GI Joe* has returned in France in his 3 3/4" (about 10 cm) [4] and stays close to the *Action Man* of 12-inches (30 cm) on the shop shelves. *Action Man* benefited from a new function in being able to talk (with lip movements). In 2004, *Action Man* is rejoined by two team members to form *Action Team*. Red Wolf, the Indian and Flynt help him to fight against the X robots that prolong the evil work of Dr. X. New adventures in synthetic images have just been edited by *Hasbro* on a promotional DVD.

After 40 years of action, *GI Joe* and *Action Man* have not finished making children dream.

---

4. It concerns the *GI Joe Vs COBRA* range. *GI Joe*'s return in France has been the subject of a dossier in the N° 21 of *Dixième Planète*.

OTHER COUNTRIES & INSPIRATION

GI Joe has known numerous 'cousins' throughout the world between the sixties and eighties and even beyond. There's been *Action Man* for Great Britain and *Action Joe* for France, as we've just seen, but also *Geyperman* for Spain, *GI Joe* for Italy, *Combat Joe* for Japan and *Action Team* for Germany.

It is worth noting that between the *Palitoy* creations for *Action Man* and the complimentary work of the Germans, Spanish and French, the *Hasbro* European licences developed an incredible independence in relation to the American range, to the point of stating that some of these new toys from across the Atlantic are still unknown to American collectors.

ACTION TEAM

Taking the initials of *GI Joe*'s *Adventure Team*, the range diffused in West Germany by *Schildkröt Spielwaren* in the seventies carried the name of *Action Team*[1]. Three quite specific members formed this team of action men. The brown John Steel[2], the bearded brown Hard Rock and the black Tom Stone. They wore civilian clothes of adventurers inspired by the American product range. First of all, they were rejoined by two girls (Super Sandy and Super Peggy), then by the Indian girl Shalaly, Bob Power and the Indian Adler Auge. Several details distinguish these German action figures. Firstly, the military sets are treated in a less warlike way. A blue beret's 'U.N.' armband accompanied most of the outfits and classic uniforms were elements of the collection 'Soldaten der Welt', (soldiers of the world), as at this epoch, West Germany was still occupied by Allied Troops. The Police motorcyclist wore of course, the green uniform of the 'Polizei' and the fireman corresponded to that of the country.

Action Team is the only range in the world to have disposed of a figure with movable eyes and a bearded blond (Bob Power). As for the *Group Action Joe*, *Action Team* counted three girls and an Indian with movable eyes (Adler Auge) identical to Oeil de Lynx. The girls are identical to the three female members of *Group Action Joe*. Super Sandy wears the same jean outfit as Jane, but her hair is auburn instead of blond. Shalaly is identical to the first version of Daïna, same for Super Peggy who is identical in every respect to the first French Peggy.

The name, *Action Team* is equally associated with *GI Joe* in Italy for the range under licence, which was largely distributed by *Polistil*.

---

1. In 2004, *Action Team* is the name of the team formed by *Action Man* and his two new allies (Red Wolf and Flynt) in Europe.
2. John Steel is the name of the celebrated American parachutist who remained caught up on the Church Bell of 'Sainte-Mère-Eglise' at the time of the Normandy Landing on the 6th June 1944.

John Steel, Super Sandy and Hard Rock, three members of Action Team. The German range had it's own identity as one can see from the packaging and catalogues of that epoch.

Above. **Geyperman** six-wheeled amphibian vehicle made in Spain between 1975 and 1980 and Geyperman modern, sound-producing helicopter manufactured by *M&C* for *Bizak* in 2002.
Opposite. **The** '*Classicos Falcon*' made in Brazil by *Estrella*.
Below. Super hero *Mego* (of which the very rare Mightor) and Lone Ranger characters with the Far West village by *Marx* and *Gabriel*.

GEYPERMAN

In Spain, a small, 17 cm action figure named *Madelman* largely inspired by *GI Joe* came to light in 1968. Created by *Manufacturas Delgado*, his name was none other than the compression of his creator's name, followed by the word 'man', made famous by *Action Man*.

The *Geyper* firm who built up a licence agreement with *Hasbro* for Spain in 1975 found it only natural to baptise its *GI Joe*: *Geyperman*. Spain greatly expanded the Far West range with new sets by *Palitoy* or *Céji Arbois*. *Geyper* also built the left-hand drive Land Rover and the six-wheeled amphibian vehicle, which were used for *Action Joe*.

Since 2002, the *Bizak* firm has re-launched the *Geyperman* toys. In fact, it concerns a special production for Spain, based on the *Power Team* range from the Hong Kong firm *M&C*. Only the packaging bears the old logo and the characters' heads are specific to the Spanish market.

77

In Latin America

After the disappearance of the last *Action Man* in 1984, we find some 'Muscle Body' action figures in Latin America carrying the *GI Joe* label in Mexico (distributed by *Lili Leydi*) and under the name of *Falcon* in Brazil (distributed by *Estrella*) about ten years ago.

In the case of *Classicos Falcon*, the bodies have been reproduced from the 1975 originals and manufactured in Brazil. Only the 'AT' logo on the belt has been replaced by that of the *Estrella* firm and the indications on the backs have been modified.

The 'Inspired'

All the international ranges that have just been mentioned have, as a common denominator, stemmed from and been adapted from the original *GI Joe* under official licence. The creation by *Hasbro*, of an action figure for boys very soon inspired the toy manufacturers and so, other action men tried to compete with Joe and his cousins.

As from 1965, the toy firm *Marx* developed a 'jointed statuette' of 12-inch representing a US soldier. It concerned Stony Smith who was nothing but a doll since his uniform is sculptured and an integral part of his body. Next, *Marx* developed Western characters, knights and Safari crews before creating some smaller 'true' action figures with numerous sets under the *Lone Ranger* licence. This range is the best known in France and was distributed in Europe by *Gabriel*. One finds more than disturbing similarities between the *Hasbro* and *Marx* accessories, like the Indian tomahawks and the Cowboy's double holster belts, which only have a tiny difference in waist size.

Ideal created it's own 12-inch action figure for boys with *Captain Action*. Ideal's approach was different, this time they were not inspired by GI's, but by the Science Fiction heroes of the sixties. *Captain Action* is a sort of chameleon who can personify Superman just as soon as Batman or Spider-Man or Flash Gordon or Buck Rogers or even the Lone Ranger. Each set was made up of each hero's uniform and his face or mask.

In the seventies, the *Mego* brand develops *Action Jackson*, a bearded adventurer, disposing him also with numerous accessories, sets and vehicles. *Action Jackson* is smaller than *GI Joe*. There follows numerous action figures derived from comic books and TV serials, with notably the super heroes from *Star Trek*, *Starsky and Hutch* and the *Planet of the Apes*. Towards the end of the seventies, *Mego* adapted it's concept to develop action figures of the same scale as *GI Joe*, with figures of James Bond from the *Moonraker* film, the *Black Hole* (a *Disney* film) or the *Star Trek* film and, of course, the super heroes like *Superman* or *Spider-man*. These toys were distributed in France by the firm, *Pim Pim Toys*, who produced a super Stone Age hero, Mightor, from the *Hanna Barbera* cartoon film, uniquely for France.

A glimpse of the very large Cherilea Toy collection.

Adventure Man advertisements and toys.

Kenner, who during our time has been integrated with the *Hasbro* Group, developed 12-inch action figures. The most celebrated is the '*Six Million Dollar Man*' who was distributed in France by *Meccano* in the second half of the seventies. In 78, *Kenner* produced the 30 cm (12-inch) figures of the *Star Wars* heroes, then the figure *Indiana Jones*[3].

In France, the best known competitor of *Action Joe* is *Mattel*'s *Big Jim* who made his appearance in 1972. With a size of 25 cm, *Big Jim* was smaller and had the particularity of being more sports-orientated than Joe.

Big Jim disappeared some years after *Action Man* in the middle of the eighties. In response to the return of *Action Man* in the nineties, *Mattel* put *Max Steel*, who is the same size as the «*biggest of all heroes*», on the market.

The Action Joe 'Imitations'

For all the numerous competitors that have been produced during Joe's reign, there existed some real toys closely inspired by his adventures. In France *Action Joe* inspired *Adventure Man* distributed by *Bertin*. Action men with 'real' hair accompanied by action girls disposing of the same sets. The resemblance between the characters and the clothes poses, moreover, a serious problem for the actual collectors as some sellers (principally on auction sites) confound the *Adventure Man* toys with the 'real' *Hasbro* licence toys. The members of *Adventure Man* used the *Cherilea Toy* vehicles that *Bertin* also distributed in France. These vehicles had been initially made, not to compete with *Action Man* and *GI Joe*, but to complete the *Hasbro* toy range, who stated that these machines were conceived for all 12-inch action figures. *Cherilea Toys* complemented perfectly the *Action Man* toy range in Europe with notably, some original armoured vehicles, a life raft, a bridge, a more streamlined helicopter or even a fireboat.

Other 'copies' of *GI Joe* were commercialised in France, notably some figures directly inspired of Ken, *Barbie*'s boyfriend, who wore poor quality military uniforms. This type of toy, destined for general stores carried many names, but the one most encountered was *Bertrand*.

The 'Heirs'

The eighties marked the disappearance of action figures for boys. *GI Joe* had become an action figure of about ten centimetres like the *Star Wars* figures from *Kenner*, for all that, after a brief period of total absence, the 12-inch action figure came back in the shops in two different ways from 1983 onwards. Firstly, by way of low-priced models destined for children with toys like *Strike Force*, which used some vehicles from *Cherilea Toys* coming to compete with the return of *Action Man* and then, by manner of action figures for collection. Since 1995, one again finds many models in by-products inspired by comic books or film characters[4]. A second market for the modern collection developed around 1999 with the militaria and richly detailed collections destined for history and uniformology enthusiasts[5]. The firm, *Dragon*, who originally specialised in military models, is the most celebrated in this field. It is followed closely by *BBI*, *21st century Toys* and many others like *Cotswold Collectibles* (who has specialised in accessories and complementary uniform elements).

It is in Asia that the greatest creativity is found at present. More and more new enterprises are created with the sole aim to produce new 12-inch action figures.

In our days, the market for the action figure of the scale 1/6 is wide and one can find toys of variable quality destined for several public sectors ranging from 4 years up to 99 years old! Films are made using these 'articulated actors'[6], firms specialise in creating personalised figures allowing everyone to have his or her 'double' in 12-inch[7]. *GI Joe* and his cousins' heirs have engendered what could well become a phenomenon of society.

---

3. *Kenner*'s figure of Indiana Jones was taken from that of Han Solo.
4. Latest news of the 12-inch action figures appears every two months in the magazine '*Dixième Planète*'.
5. These military collection figures have been made the subject of the book, 12-inch Action Figures of the Second World War in the *Histoire & Collections Editions*.
6. '*Ze Joujoux*' (*Toys at large*) by James L. Frachon, a short French film produced by *Mygale Films* in 1997.
7. Thierry Raynaud's firm *Limited Toys Design* based in Strasbourg has specialised in the production of 12-inch figures 'made-to order' or extremely limited series.

Power Team house and tower dating from 2003 and Strike Force truck dating from 1997.

INDEX

Products commercilised in France
from 1976 to end of 1981
by *Céji Arbois*

Each term corresponds to that utilised at the time of the first appearance of the reference in the the french range.
The remark 'with info booklet' corresponds to the little brochure supplied withe the sets only in 1978.

ACTION FIGURES - MAN

ref 2952	Figure adventurer, bearded, blond –1976-
ref 2953	Figure French soldier brown –1976-
	Figure Bob the soldier –1977-
ref 2999	Figure black, with beige shorts – 1976-
	Figure Sam, black with beige shorts – 1977-
ref 7566	Figure brown, bearded with blue shorts –1976-
	Figure Tom blond, bearded with shorts –1977-
ref 7597	Figure cowboy brown –1976-
	Figure Bill, the cowboy, brown –1977-
ref 7598	Figure Indian brown – 1976-
ref 7945	Figure Joe, adventurer, bearded, brown, eagle eyes – 1977-
ref 7946	Figure Œil de Lynx, black eagle eyes, bronzed body, long hair – 1977-
ref 2655	Figure Bob, movable eyes, brown with beige shorts – 1978-
	Figure Bob, eagle eyes, brown with khaki overalls – 1980-
ref 4012	Figure Sam blond, blue eagle eyes, pilot outfit – 1979- (First member of Group Action Joe with a British Action Man body)
ref 7978	Figure Sam, police motorcyclist, blond, eagle eyes –1980-
ref 7979	Figure Mark Captain Cosmos brown, eagle eyes – 1980-
ref 7930	Figure Bob, cameraman, blue eagle eyes –1980- (Bronzed body, cameraman of the Tropics)
ref 7950	Figure Sam underwater diver –1981- (Orange or black diving suit)
ref 7951	Figure Ted, Red Beret, brown, eagle eyes – 1981-
ref 7983	Figure naked, brown, painted eyes The Invincibles –1981-
ref 4466	Figure naked, bearded, blond, painted eyes, The Invincibles –1981-

BOXED ACTION FIGURES - MAN

ref 2724	All terrain vehicle: Figure brown, eagle eyes in Tropical outfit supplied with 6 wheeled vehicle –1978-
ref 3512	Centre communication radio : Mannequin barbu, Radio Communications Centre: Figure bearded, painted eyes on body of 1964 GI Joe with gripping hands, in Safari outfit supplied with talking radio and scenery – end1977-

LICENSED ACTION FIGURES - MAN

ref 2656	Figure Rahan (licence Pif Gadget) – 1978-
ref 1371	Figure Albator (not in Action Joe collections) – 1978-
ref 7973	Figure Zorro, movable eyes –1981- © Disney

ACTION FIGURES - WOMAN

ref 7867	Figure Jane – end 1976-
ref 7905	Figure Jane, new packaging – 1977-
ref 2657	Figure Jane, movable eyes, in yellow red tights – 1978-
ref 7904	Figure Peggy – 1977-
	Figure Peggy in yellow tights –1978-
ref 7947	Figure Daïna, Indian –1977-
	Figure Daïna in yellow tights – 1978-

OUTFITS AND ACCESSORIES

ref 7567	Set cowboy clothes – 1976-
	Set In the Conquest of the West – 1977- (Outfit of figure 7597)
ref 2661	Set Bill, In the conquest of the West with info booklet –1978- (Same base as 7567 with a more realistic hat, new trousers, new boots and the addition of stirrups)
ref 7568	Set Indian clothes with info booklet – 1976-
	Set On the Warpath –1977-
ref 2996	Set Maquisard clothes – 1976-
ref 2991	Set parachutist clothes – 1976-
	Set Red Beret commando with info booklet –1978-
ref 4544	Set legionnaire clothes –1976-
	Set On the Desert Trails with info booklet –1977-
ref 7570	Set secret agent 002 clothes – 1976-
ref 7594	Set American soldier clothes – 1976-
ref 7595	Set Medical Orderly clothes –1976-
	Set Operation Red Cross –1977-
ref 7569	Set Russian soldier clothes – 1976-
ref 2995	Set German soldier clothes –1976-
ref 2997	Set English soldier clothes – 1976-
ref 7018	Set German Officer clothes – 1976-
ref 7143	Set French Officer clothes –1976-
ref 2981	Set English Officer clothes –1976-
ref 2985	Set Mountain Ranger clothes (with blue fabric beret) –1976-
	Set Mountain Ranger (with hat and cartridge belt)
ref 4561	Set Leader of the Rope Party with info booklet – 1976-
ref 7123	Set and accessories Capture of the gorilla –1976-
	Coffret Capture of the gorilla with info booklet –1978-
ref 5604	Set clothes soldier In the Tropics –1976-
ref 2973	Set clothes and accessories In the Deep Seas with GI Joe comic –1976-
	Coffret In the Deep Seas with info booklet –1977-
ref 2972	Set clothes and accessories Underwater fisherman with GI Joe comic –1976- (with shark)
ref 2666	Set underwater fisherman with info booklet – 1978- (2972 without the shark)
ref 2998	clothes and accessories Secret Mission – 1976-
ref 2989	Set clothes and accessories King of the Sky – 1976-
	Coffret King of the Sky with info booklet – 1978-
ref 2665	Set Zorro with info booklet – 1978-
ref 7906	Set In the Name of the Law (Sheriff) – 1977-
ref 2664	Set Blue tunic 7e cavalry with info booklet – 1978-
ref 7910	Set Canadian Mounted Police with info booklet – 1977-

ref 7909	Set Davy Crockett – 1977-
ref 2667	Set Arctic Mission (complimentary to 2710) – 1978-
ref 7908	Set Speleologue with info booklet –1977-
ref 7911	Set State Police motorcyclist with info booklet –1977- (New helmet in 1980)
ref 2674	Special Coffret/Set Republican Guard with info booklet – 1978-
ref 7914	Set Fire Alert (Paris Fireman) with info booklet – 1977-
ref 2669	Set Sea Rescue with info booklet – 1978-
ref 2673	Set Marine Gunner with info booklet – 1978-
ref 7907	Set Safari – 1977-
ref 2670	Set French soldier with info booklet – 1978- (Outfit of figure2953)
ref 7915	Set Karate with info booklet on the martial arts – 1977-
ref 4041	Set German parachutist – 1979-
ref 4042	Set Africa Corps – 1979-
ref 4018	Set Tank Commander – 1979-
ref 4019	Set Dispatch Rider motorcyclist – 1979-
ref 4053	Set Cross-country on Motorbike with equipment – 1979-
ref 4031	Special Set Space Conquest – 1979-
ref 7976	Set Saharan Commando – 1980-
ref 7931	Set Israeli Parachutist – 1980-
ref 7937	Set American Parachutist – 1980-
ref 7938	Set Fighter Pilot – 1980-
ref 4050	Set Legionnaire Green Beret Parachutist – 1980-
ref 7948	Set Space Pirate – 1980- (Astronaut's helmet, Albator's pistol, flame thrower gun from tropics)
ref unkn.	Set Marine Swimmer (black diving suit) – 1981-
ref 7984	Set U.S. Machine gunner – 1981-
ref 7954	Set Operation Sabotage – 1981-

TWO BLISTER SHARED OUTFITS (UNIFORMS, ACCESSORIES AND WEAPONS)

ref 7575	Blister pack uniform English soldier – 1976-
ref 7576	Blister pack accessories English soldier – 1976-
ref 7577	Blister pack uniform German Officer – 1976-
ref 7578	Blister pack accessories German Officer – 1976-
ref 7579	Blister pack uniform Russian soldier – 1976-
ref 7580	Blister pack accessories Russian soldier – 1976-
ref 7581	Blister pack uniform parachutist – 1976-
ref 7582	Blister pack accessories parachutist – 1976-
ref 7583	Blister pack uniform soldier of Tropics – 1976-
ref 7584	Blister pack accessories soldier of Tropics – 1976-
ref 7585	Blister pack accessories German soldier – 1976-
ref 7586	Blister pack uniform German soldier – 1976-
ref 7587	Blister pack uniform American soldier – 1976-
ref 7588	Blister pack accessories American soldier – 1976-
ref 7591	Blister pack outfit Leader of the Rope Party – 1976-
ref 7592	Blister pack accessories Leader of the Rope Party – 1976-
ref 7589	Blister pack outfit Underwater fisherman – 1976-
ref 7590	Blister pack accessories Underwater fisherman – 1976- (Different bottles from that of set 2972)
ref 7923	Blister pack accessories Indian – 1977-
ref 7925	Blister pack outfit Indian – 1977-
ref 7926	Blister pack accessories Big Chief Indian – 1977-

ACTION FIGURES OUTFITS - WOMAN

ref 7868	Set clothes and accessories/Coffret In open Sky with info booklet – 1976-
ref 7869	Set clothes and accessories At the bottom of the seas – 1976- (With underwater electric scooter)
ref 2676	Set At the bottom of the seas with info booklet – 1978- (7869 without the scooter that will be sold apart under the Ref.2687)
ref 7870	Set clothes and accessories In the Jungle – 1976-
ref 2677	Set In the Jungle with info booklet – 1978-
ref 7871	Set clothes On the white slopes – 1976-
ref 2678	Set On the Ice floes with info booklet – 1979-
ref 2679	Set On Ranch J with info booklet – 1978-
ref 7917	Coffret Rope party in the Rockies with info booklet – 1977-
ref 2712	Set In the Sioux camp with info booklet – 1978-

TWO BLISTER SHARED OUTFITS - WOMAN

ref 7927	Outfit At the bottom of the seas – 1977-
ref 7928	Accessories At the bottom of the seas – 1977-
ref 7929	Outfit In the Jungle – 1977-
ref 7933	Outfit In open Sky – 1977-
ref 7934	Accessories Parachute – 1977-

WEAPONS AND ACCESSORIES

ref 7571	Blister pack special operation (kit) – 1976-
ref 7596	Officer's tent – 1976- Tent Operation Red Cross – 1977- Command Tent – 1981-
ref 7572	Blister pack Morse lamp – 1976-
ref 2974	Blister pack camp bed – 1976-
ref 2976	Blister pack Arms rack – 1976-
ref 2978	6(in 76) then 8 Blister packs (in 78) of arms, a ninth corresponding to the accessories of set 7570 will come to replace the gun with telescopic lens in 1981
ref 2983	Blister pack Bazooka – 1976-
ref 2975	Blister pack mortar – 1976-
ref 7090	Parachute landing container – 1976-
ref 7426	Machine gun M3 electric sound effects – 1976-
ref 5601	Machine gun electric 19cm – 1976- (luminous barrel with two sacks of sand)
ref 2711	Hammock – 1978-
ref 2682	Blister pack Rahan – 1978- (Neck-chain, dagger, spear, bow and arrows)
ref 7924	Blister pack Bridge made of liana – 1977-
ref 7936	Tepee Tent Indian – 1977-
ref 2684	Blister pack Polar Mission – 1978- (snowshoes and small sledge)
ref 2710	Polar expedition – 1978- (Sledge, team of two dogs, canteen and cord)
ref 7913	Blister pack Inflatable boat – 1977- (With removable paddle, container and compass)
ref 7943	Blister pack accessories firemen – 1977- (Water hose extinguisher and whistle completing the set 7914)
ref 2687	Blister pack underwater scooter with electric motor – 1978- (Same as that which was supplied in 1976 with the set 7869)
ref 2726	Blister pack Kalashnikov machine gun – 1978-
ref 2728	Blister pack XM 24 machine gun – 1978-
ref 2727	Blister pack infra-rouge gun – 1978-
ref 2729	Blister pack Lewis machine gun – 1978-
ref 4047	Blister pack cover and rails for trailer 4043 – 1979-
ref 4034	Search light big exercises – 1979- (Used alone or with 4562,4043 and 2749/7972)
ref 7980	Light canon 105mm – 1980- (can be towed by 4562 and fire shells)
ref 7981	Blister pack laser gun – 1980- (luminous lights up on the 7965)
ref 7965	Blister pack Electricity generator – 1980- (Battery harness)
ref 7968	Blister pack ultrasounds radar – 1980- (lights up on the 7965)
ref 7967	Blister pack turbocopter – 1980- (lights up on the 7965)
ref unkn.	Blister pack Arsenal N° 1 – 1981-
ref unkn.	Blister pack Arsenal N° 2 – 1981- (Regroup 2729 and arms 2978)
ref unkn.	Blister pack sabotage material – 1981-

ref unkn. (English gas mask, detonator, radio, grenades, dynamite, binoculars, pistol, rocket launcher and a hand searchlight)
Blister pack Free First Aid kit offered with game competition " Operation Niagara " –1982-

ANIMALS

ref 4541	Horse – 1976- (Light coloured version with cowboy saddlery)
ref 7960	Mustang – 1977- (Articulated horse)
ref 7919	Giant spider in blister pack – 1977-
ref 7920	Two snakes in blister pack – 1977- (One green and a mottled viper)
ref 7921	Crocodile in blister pack –1977-
ref 7922	Articulated eagle in blister pack – 1977-
ref 2710	Polar Expedition – 1978- (Two dogs with sledge, canteen and cord)

VEHICLES

ref 4559	Helicopter yelow – 1976- green –1977-
ref 2986	Assault dinghy with electric motor – 1976-
ref 4562	Land-Rover –1976-
ref 7830	Training tower for shop window display – 1976-
ref 7903	Training tower – 1977-
ref 2742	Motorbike – 1978-
ref 2715	Motorbike sidecar with machine gun – 1978- (2742 with sidecar)
ref 7942	Bathyscaph – 1977-
ref 2744	Scorpion Tank – 1978-
ref 2724	Jeep: Figure brown, movable eyes in tropical outfit supplied with 6-wheeled vehicle – 1979-
ref 2749	Fighter electric vehicle four-wheel drive – 1978- (From the Joustra model Dune cruiser)
ref 7941	Delta wing – 1977-
ref 2725	Canoe – 1978-(To decorate in Indian or Trapper version and descent of rapids)
ref 4043	Campaign Trailer – 1979-
ref 4033	(To complete with blister pack accessories 4047) Small amphibious all-purpose tracked vehicle – 1979- (Same model as 2724 with tracks, windscreen and snow camouflage)
ref 4046	Capture Copter – 1979- (4559 black with floats, a claw and an armoured canopy)
ref 4044	Cross-country motorbike – 1979- (Five different colours)
ref 7972	4 x 4 Commando (camouflage version of 2749) – 1980-
ref 2967	All-purpose trapper (6 wheeled troop transporter)
ref 2966	Condor F.X.001 (Four vehicles in one) – 1979-
ref 7982	Radian –1980- (Spaceship with sound effects and flashing laser beam)
ref 7974	Stratos Remote controlled – 1980- (Seems to have never been commercialised)
ref 7975	Stratos electric – 1980- (7974 motorised without remote control)
ref 7987	State Police motorbike – 1981-

SPECIAL OFFER PACKS

ref 3811	Tepee + Indian figure – 1981-
ref 3812	Canoe + Indian figure – 1981-
ref 4236	Tom in box + two Western outfits – 1981-

GAME ACCESSORIES

ref 7831	Empty suitcase – 1976-
ref 7593	Empty wooden canteen – 1976-
ref 7518	Amplified Morse Radio LW– 1976-
ref 7680	Military Radio LW – MW – 1976-
ref 7720	Walkie -Talkie 5 T – 1976-
ref 7902	4 audiocassettes sold separately – 1977-